Communication Skills for Surviving Conflicts at Work

Janice Walker Anderson
SUNY-New Paltz
Myrna Foster-Kuehn
Clarion State University
Bruce Converse McKinney
University of North Carolina-Wilmington

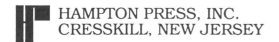

HAMPTON PRESS, INC.
CRESSKILL, NEW JERSEY

Printed in the United States of America

Library of Congress Cataloging-in-Publication Data

Anderson, Janice Walker.
    Communication skills for surviving conflicts at work /
Janice Walker Anderson, Myrna Foster-Kuehn, Bruce
Converse McKinney.
        p. cm.
    Includes bibliographic references and index.
    ISBN 1-57273-056-0 (cloth). -- ISBN 1-57273-057-9 (paper)
    1. Conflict management. 2. Communication in management.
3. Interpersonal communication.   I. Foster-Kuehn, Myrna.
II. McKinney, Bruce C. III. Title.
HD42.A523   1996
650.1'3--dc20   96-3
                                                          CIP

Image of the "Anja Chakra" on the front cover reprinted from *Pranic
Healing*, 1990, York Beach, Maine: Samuel Weiser, Inc., p. 109.
Reprinted with permission of the author, Choa Kok Sui.

Hampton Press, Inc.
23 Broadway
Cresskill, NJ 07626

Contents

Preface

So often, it seems that conflicts spring up and hit us smack between the eyebrows, surprising us with high energy levels and unexpected interactions. That is why the image on the cover of this book is so appropriate. According to Master Choa Kok Sui, the image depicts the energy (chi) center (Anja Chakra) located between the eyebrows that controls through the pituitary gland the body's endocrine system. When this energy center is activated, it energizes the whole body.

Conflict has a similar effect, energizing people, whether for good or for ill. A natural part of organizational life, conflicts at work can stimulate creative problem solving, increase job commitment, and prompt organizational change. All too often, however, conflicts become destructive, distorting communication patters and creating stress for all involved. In this book, we provide practical suggestions for discovering the constructive potentials in the chaos of conflict interactions.

Our goal is to blend theory and practice to provide a richer understanding of the conflict process, allowing you to make more informed choices about what is under your control during conflict episodes—your own responses. While you cannot control the conflict process, you can manage your own talk in ways that increase the likelihood of creating productive outcomes, maintaining your working relationships, and preserving your sanity. By understanding the nature of conflict interactions, you can exercise your right to make ethical choices that are consistent with your personal values and career goals. Whether you are facing conflicts as a subordinate, as a member of a work unit, or as a supervisor, this book will help you to recognize the signs of trouble, anticipate how conflict episodes might unfold, and devise flexible and appropriate strategies for coping. It is our hope that this book will be of interest to professionals as well as to students.

We would like to gratefully acknowledge the contributions of the people who either directly or indirectly helped us in completing this book. We are indebted to Barbara Bernstein at Hampton Press for her support. We would also like to acknowledge the students in our classes whose questions motivated our interest in conflict and whose unfailingly honest and straightforward responses to our manuscript served as our rudder of readability. We must acknowledge as well our colleagues at our home institutions who managed to coexist with us during the writing of this manuscript.

Finally, we would like to dedicate this book to the memory of Gerald M. Phillips, our teacher and mentor, who taught us some of our most important lessons in conflict. He was a distinguished scholar and a dedicated teacher whose irascible style and practical wisdom will be sorely missed.

Janice W. Anderson, Ph.D.
SUNY-New Paltz

Myrna Foster-Kuehn
Clarion State University

Bruce Converse McKinney
University of North Carolina-Wilmington

▶ 1

Putting Conflict in Perspective

INTRODUCTION

There are a wide variety of ways to manage or resolve conflict. Inspector Callahan, the police officer in the "Dirty Harry" movies, had a highly effective way of immediately resolving conflict situations. "Go ahead, make my day" has become a stock phrase to express a tough, determined, and absolutely able-to-win attitude. It's a fun fantasy—achieving victorious results, immediate respect (of a sort), and instant adoration from all the "victims" of the world; but nevertheless, it is only a fantasy. *Productive* conflict management depends on achieving results that do not cause physical harm to others or yourself, land you in jail, or otherwise end your professional career.

1

Achieving this goal is quite difficult because conflict appears in so many different forms. It can spring up quickly and unannounced; it can grow into monstrous proportions over a long period of time; it can be tame and easily handled. This chapter is designed to help you recognize how "IT" comes about. People who have less trouble dealing with conflict have learned how to recognize the signs of trouble, predict the way conflict will develop, and assess the various factors that determine an appropriate response to conflict. The material covered in this chapter focuses on how you can develop these insights. We answer such basic questions as: What is conflict? What causes it? How can you tell when the pain is worth it?

THE FEAR AND LOATHING OF CONFLICT

Conflict at work is a common occurrence, yet most of us go to great lengths to avoid facing our differing and competing perspectives. We fear that only destructive outcomes can result from acknowledging our differences with those around us. All too often, conflict is marked by hostility and/or verbal aggression. We are all familiar with the emotional costs of conflict interaction. Because conflict episodes are probably the most threatening and stressful circumstances we face at work, we tend to avoid facing the issues until the pressure builds to a climax.

People are often reluctant to face serious issues because they are anxious or ignorant about how to respond effectively. Although some problems do indeed "just go away," truly significant issues are heightened by this type of neglect. Conflict will surface one way or another until the issues are resolved or the relationships change. In the following case study, notice how the unresolved issue of defining productivity levels created conflict that rippled down through the organizational hierarchy until it touched even new arrivals.

Case Study 1.1: The Trainee and the Overworked Manager

Connor Blake was just getting ready to start his morning work at the JANCO corporation when a new employee, Gene Foster, arrived. Gene explained that he was there to familiarize himself with a particular machine before reporting to his designated weekend shift. Gene's training period (to take place during Connor's shift) was to last two weeks.

Gene and Connor were getting acquainted when the shift manager, Pat Stuart, walked in. Pat was in an unusually irate mood for such an early hour of the morning. He proceeded, without even giving a perfunctory greeting to either worker, to question the newly arrived trainee. "Who are you?" he asked. Gene politely answered, "Gene Foster, sir." "Well," replied the manager, "Mr. Foster, what the hell are you doing here?!" The sentence was clipped, cold, and aggressive. Gene nevertheless proceeded to repeat what he had explained to Connor. As he spoke, Pat seemed to become more and more agitated and finally cut Gene off in mid-sentence, "Do you seriously think I have the time to train you?!" This was obviously not a question. Gene was taken aback. He began, "But . . ." and was cut off again. Pat exploded, "There are no 'buts'! I have production deadlines and there's no way in hell I'm going to mobilize one man and one machine simply to train you—who won't even remain on my shift!"

By then, Gene was more than uncomfortable, reeling in confusion as well as fright. This was not what he had expected when he was told to report for work. He stood in front of his new manager, motionless, not daring to look Pat in the face. Pat, on the other hand, was not talking as loudly, but remained cold and authoritative as he pursued his argument. "We can't complete this production run on schedule if we are down one person and one machine," he continued.

Connor tried to intervene on Gene's behalf. He pointed out to Pat that Gene was new there (hinting that a calmer tone of voice would be more appropriate) and suggested that he could train Gene without loosing production time. Needless to say, Connor never made it to the end of his suggestions. He was promptly silenced by Pat's dry, "Who asked you?" By interrupting the manager, however, Connor gave Gene a chance to regroup and ask Pat what he was supposed to do. Pat replied, "Do whatever you want, but my department will not train you," and stormed out of the room.

After Pat's departure, Gene exploded, "I have never been treated in this manner!" "What is this, the army?" he raged. He was obviously hurt and extremely worried about his job. Gene decided to call Pat's boss; then he, too, stormed out of the room.

Gene returned about 15 minutes later, wearing a self-satisfied grin. He explained to Connor that the boss would call Pat to straighten things out. Gene and Connor continued to discuss the incident. Connor tried to explain that Pat was not really a bad person and that the department had been under tremendous pressure recently. His effort was to no avail. Gene had already rebaptized Pat "The Asshole."

Pat finally stormed back in. "You," he simply said, pointing at Gene. He was making an obvious effort to control his anger. He explained that Connor would train Gene, who was staring defiantly at Pat but remaining verbally polite, interjecting "yes, sir" every time he had the chance. Pat pointed out that he didn't like "people who are just out to get what they want." He added, "Next time, observe protocol and talk to me about your problems. There's no reason why we shouldn't be able to work things out." With that, he marched out muttering something under his breath.

"Yeah, right!" Gene snapped as the door closed behind Pat, "Tell me something I'll believe." Turning to Connor he said, "I really nailed him, didn't I?" Connor didn't answer, changing the subject to get started with the training. Connor knew this was not the end.

Pat had exploded at the newly arrived trainee with no apparent provocation. Was Pat actually addressing the person toward whom he felt angry? Were his actions effective in helping him deal with production levels? How did Gene's emotional decision to call Pat's supervisor add a new dimension to the original conflict? What could be the effect of Gene's "tattling to the boss"? How do you think Connor felt after this episode? Rather than resolve issues, this interaction complicated the problem and set the stage for continued conflict.

Obviously, underlying problems within the organization stimulated this interaction. In this case, as in many workplace conflicts, the tensions were not confined to two individuals. Instead, the conflict spread to include subordinates and supervisors, becoming more tangled and complex as it touched more people.

It is easy to see why *persistent conflicts reduce productivity*, sometimes emerging indirectly through absenteeism, high turnover, and work-to-rule environments. Everyone involved is likely to feel less job satisfaction and organizational commitment. When people suppress feelings of tension and discontent, their communication becomes unreliable—they distort information and restrict what they say, creating fertile grounds for misinterpretations (not to mention bad judgments about what actions to take). Conflicts at work combine high energy levels with antagonistic attitudes, producing a volatile climate in which innovation is severely hampered (Neale & Bazerman, 1991).

Ironically, the opposite is also true. *Conflict, when handled properly, is a catalyst for change*, stimulating creative problem solving and cementing interpersonal relationships among those who chose to work through their differences. In the process of working through differences, people search out a broader range of information and consider alternative solutions. Better decision making can result as blind spots are identified. Pulling together in the face of adversity can energize a work unit as boundaries are defined more clearly—employees can thus develop stronger bonds through the process of creating common ground. Finally, conflict can signal underlying problems within an organization and function as a safety valve, providing an outlet for frustrations (Neale & Bazerman, 1991).

The problem is not that people disagree; it's how they manage their disagreements. Rather than viewing conflict as something to be removed, in this book we focus on how to channel the energy created by the spark of differences. It is the way that people in conflict situations manage their behaviors that determines how constructive (or destructive) the conflict will be.

GETTING A HANDLE ON CONFLICT

In dealing with conflict, it is essential to understand not only what it is, but what it *isn't*. There are several common myths that people bring to conflict situations. We address common misconceptions (myths) about workplace conflicts, and then offer our definition of conflict.

What Conflict Isn't

Myth #1: Conflict is unnatural. Peace is the natural state of human affairs. Do you believe that harmony in the workplace is the status quo and that conflict is a disruption in an otherwise peaceful environment? Do you feel that it is your responsibility to maintain order in your organization so that everyone gets along? Whenever there is conflict, do you believe that something is wrong? As Hocker and Wilmot (1991) pointed out, "Conflict is not a temporary aberration. It alternates with harmony in an ebb and flow pattern" (p. 8). When you consider the number of individuals in your organization with different values, skills, educational levels, and ethnic and religious backgrounds, you may begin to understand why peace is more of an abnormal state of human affairs than is conflict.

Myth #2: In the management of conflict, there is a winner and a loser. This is probably the most damaging myth regarding conflict because it keeps many people from trying to end a dispute; they fear that they may be the "loser." As Hocker and Wilmot (1991) noted, the metaphors we use to discuss conflict draw on battle field images: We speak of "shooting down" another's argument or "destroying" the "other's" claims. These simple war-like terms encourage strategic manipulation and can become self-fulfilling prophecies, leading us to focus on winning and to ignore the relationships between people who must continue to interact with one another on a day-to-day basis.

In focusing on short-term gains, we can lose sight of the long-term losses involved in damaged work relationships. What is essential to keep in mind during conflict interaction is that our very differences can provide the basis for mutual gains. By coordinating interpretations, *both* parties can come away feeling as if they have won.

Myth #3: Conflicts develop because of inadequate information. Most typically, it's not that information is lacking; it's that people don't make good use of the information available to them. Managers often make very poor use of the information available to them about human motivation and communication; they want productivity, but are reluctant or unable to do what is necessary with their employees. Conflict management involves a lot of work in uncharted territories, and work in emotionally charged areas is uncomfortable for managers who like quick, predictable actions (Butt, 1990).

Myth #4: People are well trained for handling conflicts on the job. Whereas, technical expertise is usually a given factor in job placement, most people are poorly trained in other aspects of their jobs such as planning, organizing, and exercising power. Much less attention is typically devoted to the nuances of leadership, team building, and conflict management. When it comes to conflict, we must pick things up "on the job." However, we expect others to function effectively during times of stress despite the fact that they are being asked to perform outside of their areas of technical expertise.

Myth #5: Conflicts could be avoided if people would just act rationally. Most of us would like to think that we respond intellectually, intelligently, and objectively on the job to issues, people, and situations. Hocker and Wilmot (1985) noted that people who engage in conflict are often seen as hostile, neurotic, and anti-social. The emotions called forth in conflict episodes are viewed as deviations from rationality and, consequently, individuals are encouraged to veil their true feelings, to separate the people from the problem.

Ignoring emotions during conflict, however, is unrealistic. Conflict is seldom an intellectual exercise between strangers of weighing the pros and cons of an issue. It's usually something that happens between people with a common bond, and it's usually taken quite personally. To deny emotions is to ignore the important role they play in building relationships and a sense of community. "Emotions are key factors," Putnam and Mumby (1992) wrote, "in forming mutual understanding by cuing empathy, gaining insights into expectations, building shared interpretations and understanding life histories" (p. 22).

Rather than dismiss sincere emotions as being counterproductive, we should accept them as an integral factor in the conflict process, providing touchstones of genuineness that point to areas of real needs. "Rational" is actually a value-laden term; its meaning depends on your perspective. The people and the problem are not so easily separated, and we have to use both our hearts and our minds in managing conflict.

Myth #6: Conflict is the result of personality clashes. This myth, identified by Hocker and Wilmot (1985), refers to the idea that managers often try to resolve conflict in a parental way, assuming that some people are just difficult to get along with. What this myth does not address is that conflict is frequently a symptom of systemic problems, not the result of personalities. "When people are simply separated from each other, or isolated from the larger group, in the hope that they will not bother the rest of the group, usually the conflict worsens" (p. 9).

All too often in the conflict process, organizational problems remain hidden beneath the explicit behaviors of individuals. Instead of declaring a winner and loser, Pat's boss might have recognized the outburst as a symptom of underlying problems with work load issues. Although many managers recognize this general principle, they seldom apply it in dealing with actual conflicts. Frequently, managers prefer to blame individuals and avoid dealing with the broader, more difficult problems in the system.

Myth #7: Conflict is just a communication breakdown. Simons (1986) found that people often use the phrase "communication breakdown" when discussing a conflict or disagreement.

This term incorrectly implies noncommunication; the reality is that there is a breakdown in understanding, not communication. Deutsch (1969), for example, found that people placed little confidence in information obtained directly from the other party in a conflict situation, expecting espionage and other circuitous or devious means of obtaining information. All too often, our communication in conflict episodes focuses on undermining the position of the other person, not on identifying what their real needs are. Poor communication practices enhance the possibility of error and misinformation of the sort that is likely to reinforce negative conflict dynamics. Talking without understanding is not a panacea. Unless disputants in a conflict understand good conflict-management skills, their attempts to "communicate" may only lead to greater frustration.

Myth #8: People can confront all conflicts. People at work do not have the luxury of unlimited time and energy. Individuals who go about confronting every issue without regard to the value or importance of the issue may impede their own and others' productivity. You need to decide when confrontation is appropriate and when it is better to avoid making the differences explicit.

What Conflict Is

The common thread that runs through definitions of conflict behavior is *incompatible goals*—"If you get what you want, I can't get what I want." Deutsch (1973) argued that conflict "exists whenever incompatible activities occur" (p. 10). Kerr (1964) saw conflict as an attempt by one party to injure, thwart, or control the behavior of another. On the most basic level, conflict involves incompatible goals and limited resources.

Such definitions describe conflict behavior in terms of objective "facts" external to the people involved in the process. Conflict is "objectified" by defining it as a struggle over events, issues, or objects. Although incompatible goals are an everyday occurrence in modern organizations faced with turbulent environments and downsizing, it is also true that incompatibility can be as much a matter of perception as an objective fact.

Defining conflict simply in terms of incompatible goals assumes that the issues are clear and that the parties involved have a common understanding of the nature of the problem. Although conflict interaction involves dealing with *real differences of interests*, conflict is motivated as much by our *perceptions* of incompatibility as it is by the objective reality of scarce resources (Folger & Poole, 1984). Our actions and reactions are based on personal interpretations of objective circumstances. Our beliefs about the world and about the "other" involved in a conflict play an important role in shaping our strategic choices in the conflict process.

In our case study, according to the way the shift manager, Pat, saw it, he and the new trainee, Gene, had incompatible goals. If Gene "won" his training, Pat "lost" his productivity. This definition of the conflict obscured the fact that a trainee could be an additional body to help relieve the load of the department. Pat was only concerned with the short-term success of his shift that week. His assumption that trainees were useless led him to ignore ways in which he might have turned the liability of a trainee into an asset.

Interdependence is another key aspect of conflict situations. If the parties involved in a conflict don't need each other on some level, they could just walk away. Conflicts involve mixed motives; an urge to compete is combined with a need to cooperate. This duality is a constant theme, and it helps explain why conflict interaction can be so confusing. There are usually a variety of sometimes contradictory reasons for people's actions—the variety of motives operating during any conflict episode makes interpreting the meaning of an action difficult.

Yet another key aspect of *conflict involves specific behaviors people engage in* as they interact. Focusing on the way people manage their talk during conflict episodes helps you concentrate on tangible behaviors rather than on intangible personality traits. It helps you avoid the distortion that occurs when you try to be a mind reader, when you make inferences about how the "other" feels about the situation or about you. Defining conflict episodes in terms of specific behaviors makes the process less mysterious and helps you describe how things could be different—behaviors are much easier to change than personalities.

The definitions we have explored here highlight that conflict is a combination of:

- interdependent individuals
- who perceive incompatible goals
- and interact in order to
- gain something of value to them.

This seems fairly simple . . . but the reality of dealing with conflict is often complex and confusing. It's helpful to understand the variety of factors encouraging conflict in the workplace.

UNDERSTANDING WHAT CAUSES CONFLICT

At the heart of any conflict is a feeling of tension. Webster's dictionary defines *tension* as "inner unrest, striving, or imbalance: a feeling of psychological stress often manifested by increased muscle tonus or by other physiological indications of emotion." Tension develops as our perceptions about the world are called into question by the clash of differences. On the most basic level, conflict interaction implies questioning ourselves as we strive to coordinate our value systems with those of others. This tension, that is both physiological and psychological, has a number of causes. We discuss both individual and organizational causes of conflict.

Individual Causes of Conflict

Getting a handle on conflict requires taking a look at both the issues and the way people respond to them. It helps to understand some of the factors that can motivate "good" people to engage in destructive behaviors toward themselves or others. The individual roots of conflict spring from our need for balance, our tendency to mirror behavior, and our need to release psychic energy.

Need for consistency. Consistency theorists Heider (1946), Osgood and Tannenbaum (1955), and Festinger (1957, 1964) argued that people have an inherent *need for cognitive balance*— for consistency between their thoughts (or cognitions) and their actions in external reality. If this balance is upset, psychological tension results. This explains why most people have a hard time making friendly chit-chat with people they hate.

We can react in a number of different ways to reduce this tension. Research has indicated, for example, that we may: (a) denigrate the source of inconsistent information, (b) decide that the disagreement is not very important or minimize it in some other way, (c) seek social support or supportive evidence for our own viewpoint, (d) misperceive the source's position, (e) ignore or forget that the cognitions are different, (f) attempt to convince the other person of their error, and/or (g) change our own position on the issues (Simons, 1986).

Consider Brian's dilemma. Brian's boss, Tina, promised him that he would have first choice of a vacation slot. Brian had already picked a great place to vacation and eagerly awaited the approval of his request for two weeks in August. When Brian found out that Tina promised those same two weeks to another person in the office with less seniority, he was extremely upset with her. He felt betrayed because he liked Tina and felt that up to that point in time they had a good working relationship.

According to the consistency principle, Brian is motivated to change some of his ideas to produce a more consistent view and relieve the tension. In the example, Brian might change his position on the best vacation time and decide that he prefers two weeks in September. He might denigrate the source, changing his feelings about Tina, and decide she really isn't that great of a boss after all. Or, he might try to convince Tina of the error of her ways.

The concept of maintaining consistency shows us that the longer two individuals who initially like each other hold opposing viewpoints on crucial issues, the greater the pressure they are under to feel hostility for each other. In other words, in order to maintain cognitive balance when you are consistently in conflict with another person, you will tend to change your view of that "other," to decide that they are not a person that you like. *You shift from disagreeing on an issue to disliking the person.*

This fact has direct implications for organizational members placed in the formal role of devil's advocate (i.e., quality-control people whose job it is to find the mistakes of others). Over time, the distinction between the individual and his or her role will be harder to maintain. From a managerial perspective, the interpersonal consequences of such formal "devil's advocate" positions need to be acknowledged and mechanisms for dealing with these reactions must be developed (i.e., rotating the role on a periodic basis).

Tendency to mirror behavior. Interpersonal reflexes also play a role in setting the stage for conflict interaction. People tend to mirror the behavior that they see, or "do unto others as you think they have done unto you." Evaluative comments prompt strong emotional responses of defense. Pat's comment, "Who the hell are you?", was sure to produce a defensive reaction. The argument escalated as the disputants tried to defend themselves by responding in kind to what they perceived to be personal attacks. The point regarding training and production levels was lost as each individual mirrored the others' tactics. In this unconscious mirroring process, each person expanded the conflict. Throughout this book, we suggest that you try to avoid unconsciously responding in kind to the other side. When you mirror their behavior, you have allowed them to control you, often without realizing it.

Need to release psychic energy. The human mind, as Freud postulated, is a reservoir of psychic energy that is channeled into various activities. Energy, such as the tension produced by conflict, must be released in some form. If it is not released through one channel, it will find its way out through another. Everyone adopts one strategy or another for channeling the energy created by the conflict process.

Psychodynamics, or the systematic study of personality and motivation, deals with how people make these choices. Some people make conscious efforts to release their anxiety by playing a challenging game of racquetball on their lunch hour or after work. Others may not consciously choose a channel for releasing the pent-up energy caused by conflict interactions. Anxiety and aggression can emerge in *indirect* ways as we suppress our feelings, displace them onto more vulnerable targets, or become frozen in compulsive behavior.

Suppressed aggression can erupt violently at unexpected times. We all shudder at the occasional horror stories of unbalanced workers attempting to settle workplace grievances with the help of a shotgun. Such reactions are extreme, but they illustrate how suppressed aggression tends to become stronger until even trivial events can precipitate an outburst. The photocopier machine breaks down one too many times and serves as the trigger for an individual's tirade about the lack of administrative support. When the intensity of the emotional reaction appears out of proportion to the immediately precipitating incident, it is a sign that deeper, more important concerns have been suppressed.

Suppressed aggression can emerge through less obvious means. You "forget" that report that your supervisor needs, or you miss a key meeting scheduled by the project team. Sometimes aggression is redirected onto a more vulnerable or acceptable target, displacing anger onto a scapegoat. The angry, frustrated executive goes home and kicks the dog. It was easier for the shift manager to yell at the new trainee than it was for him to express his frustration at the true source—his boss' production quotas. All too often, job frustrations are displaced onto others rather than being directed toward the actual source of frustration in the work environment.

Whether we acknowledge it or not, conflict involves our most basic values, and this is why we become so emotionally involved during conflict episodes. Throughout this book, we argue that effective conflict management involves recognizing that the people are inseparable from the "problem." In our case study, who would blame Gene for being insulted by: "Who are you?" and

"What the hell are you doing here?" These feelings played a large part in how Gene responded to the situation, yet he suppressed these feelings, only to act on them later.

Repetitive cycles of conflict can be broken by an individual who challenges the norm of silence about genuine emotions and honestly acknowledges his or her feelings in an appropriate and constructive fashion. It would not have served Gene well had he shouted back at his manager, "You hurt my feelings!" Constructive conflict interaction does, however, involve finding outlets for the legitimate emotions evoked in the conflict process rather than forcing these feelings to remain beneath the surface of interaction in the name of maintaining "professionalism."

In his role as a new trainee, Gene could have said, "I'm confused and overwhelmed by your response. The second level manager said I should report here. Should I call him to see where he wants me to train?" By articulating his feelings and confronting Pat with the alternative he had in mind, Gene could have illustrated to Pat the consequences of his actions, removing the sense that Gene was going behind his manager's back in calling the boss.

Psychodynamic theory helps explain why we can become locked in destructive conflict interaction cycles. One response to anxiety is to "freeze" and become inflexible, just as Pat did in our case study. A person's fears lead to a search for certainty, for control. Repeating even unpleasant behavior can be reinforcing because it provides a sense of mastery. It provides a sense of control over the situation, even if that control is focused on negative behaviors—at least the outcome is expected and predictable.

People are also motivated to act in certain ways during conflict by the need to protect their egos. Face-saving behavior can perpetuate the conflict dynamics as individuals become concerned with not appearing weak or foolish. When ego is a concern, the focus of the conflict interaction shifts from issues to relationship concerns. Gene, a new employee, was particularly concerned with his image and position in an unfamiliar hierarchy. His immediate interest in establishing the ground rules for his work relationships took precedence over longer term concerns about jumping over the supervisor's head to a higher authority. Once face-saving becomes a concern, no progress can be made on substantive issues until the relationships have been clarified.

A key part of managing conflict is identifying your stress reactions and directing your feelings toward the actual source of your stress. In chapter 2, we discuss how you can come to grips with your own reactions to conflict situations. We discuss skills that are helpful to you when conflict is sudden and unexpected, as it was for Gene, as well as when you have a chance to prepare for a specific conflict situation.

Organizational Causes of Conflict

All too often, people fall into a game of "Why don't you and him or her fight" without understanding that the organization's typical procedures are the real problem. In our case study, Pat and Gene were pitted against each other by the organization. As shift manager, Pat had to ensure that production levels remained high. The Human Resources Department assigned Gene to Pat's area because of access to specialized equipment without regard to how this action might affect short-term productivity. No one was clear about who was really "in charge" of trainees. As is so often the case, the left hand didn't know or care what the right hand was doing. In the next sections, we discuss three common organizational causes of conflict: ambiguous authority; scarce resources; and specialized roles and cultural differences.

Ambiguous lines of authority. Ambiguous lines of authority encouraged the conflict between Gene and his training supervisor, Pat. Who was responsible for trainees—their eventual line supervisors, their training managers, the second-level manager, or no one? Not knowing who is in charge can easily create conflicts among coworkers.

However, organizations frequently create such ambiguous lines of authority when they use project teams that combine product and functional managers to handle complex projects that break new ground. Although project teams benefit from the input of members from different areas of specialty, they can also suffer from vague goals and lack of consensus on the criteria for evaluating decisions. In such instances, conflict is likely to develop.

In chapter 3, we focus on conflict within work teams, explaining steps you can take as a group member to minimize the frequency of destructive conflict. We describe what constitutes effective decision making and provide suggestions for developing a sense of group identity independent from the dictates of management. We conclude by offering ideas for how you might respond in meetings to individuals such as Pat who tend to "explode" in public settings.

Project teams are not the only instances in which lines of jurisdiction and departmental responsibilities are unclear.

Periods of rapid change, whether precipitated by growth or downsizing, also create ambiguity about goals. "There is no way to steer or obtain feedback on an approach to a vague target," Brown and Agnew explained (quoted by Frank & Brownell, 1989, p. 490). Power struggles emerge in such contexts as people jockey for advantages. Ambiguous goals can provide the maneuvering room for movement toward a common goal even though individuals might have different reasons for supporting the objective. All too often, however, ambiguity results in political infighting.

In chapter 4, we explain a number of informal strategies for dealing with political machinations and define what power is, where it comes from, and when different strategies might be appropriate. We then consider the problems inherent in positions of strength and weakness, and conclude by summarizing how effective managers use power.

Scarce resources. Scarce resources are one of the most frequently mentioned reasons behind conflict behavior. The intensity of the conflict depends on the perceived incompatibilities between the parties involved. As we have mentioned, perceptions are an important part of the conflict process, leading us to focus our attention on some behaviors and ignore others. However, in some instances we really do desire things that cannot be shared.

When scarce resources need to be allocated, more formal methods of conflict management are appropriate. Chapter 5 examines one of the most common formal methods of conflict management—negotiation. Chapter 6 continues our discussion of formal dispute resolution techniques, describing third-party interventions such as mediation, arbitration, and litigation.

Specialized roles and cultural differences. "As a result of successfully adapting to their roles in the organization, people develop perceptual sets which keep them from easily understanding the perceptual sets of others," Conrad (1985, p. 49) explained. Our specialized organizational roles encourage us to interpret information solely in light of our narrow specialties. A financial analyst looking at the feasibility of a plant closing, for example, learns to focus only on the short-term economic consequences of the action without looking at the human-resources or public-relations impact of a plant closing.

Specialized roles lead individuals to develop different priorities, different time frames for considering issues, and different technical jargon for communicating. Despite these differences, however, most people tend to assume that their perceptions and needs will be clear to others. In reality, such clarity of understanding across specialized functions is highly unlikely.

Conflict becomes even more likely when cultural differences compound the differences created by specialized roles. In chapter 7 we consider how cultural differences complicate the conflict process. We attempt to help you recognize the implicit cultural assumptions that you bring to the conflict process and discuss both how to manage cultural differences across national boundaries as well as how to manage differences between co-cultures within an organization.

Understanding the variety of factors creating conflict helps you recognize why conflict episodes can be so complex and apparently contradictory. To conclude this chapter, we consider how you can distinguish constructive conflicts from destructive ones.

DETERMINING WHEN THE PAIN PAYS OFF

Managing conflict is a matter of balancing the paradox that conflict is both functional and dysfunctional. How can we tell when the pain is worth it? This question is a difficult one that eludes complete answers. We can, however, identify a number of the pieces of the puzzle that must fit together in order for conflict interaction to serve productive ends.

Look at Perceived Outcomes

The way people view their conflict interaction plays a large role in determining its productivity. During a conflict episode, people tend to focus on the negative aspects of the immediate stress they feel in the interaction. It is only afterward that they can explore the positive results of the clash of interests. People's perceptions of the usefulness of conflict change over the course of time, becoming more positive after, rather than during, the interaction. Looking back on a conflict, many people perceive the positive outcomes and minimize the stress it took to accomplish these changes.

A basic rule of thumb in assessing the productiveness of conflict is to say that productive conflict produces adaptation and change rather than stagnation and gridlock. More specifically, we can say that *conflict is constructive if it*:

- focuses attention on problems inhibiting performance;
- forces the reexamination of current goals, policies, or practices;
- energizes staff by actively involving them in the life of the organization;
- brings individuals' reservations and objections out into the open;
- generates new ideas and new perspectives;
- provokes an evaluation of organizational structure or design.

Conversely, conflict *is destructive if it*:

- continues even after a decision is hammered out;
- adversaries remain the same even when the issues change;
- outside parties get drawn into the debate;
- discussion never moves from complaints to solutions;
- one person or faction is bound and determined to emerge victorious (Neale & Bazerman, 1991).

According to these standards, the conflict in our case study was clearly destructive.

Look at Actual Interactions

If you do not have the benefit of hindsight, how can you tell if the interaction is spiraling out of control? What actual interaction patterns during a conflict episode have the greatest chance of turning the conflict in productive directions? We devote the rest of the book to helping you answer these questions.

For now, we just emphasize that productive conflict is marked by *flexibility* rather than rigidity. Constructive conflict is characterized by movement between different types of behaviors. If you find yourself repeating the same cycles, try changing your strategies in unexpected directions. Rather than repeating ineffective behaviors, look for ways to act that are different from previous patterns—changing your behaviors might stimulate new ones. Effective conflict management involves recognizing patterns of interaction and varying your responses accordingly.

SUMMARY

Most people do not enjoy facing conflict because it can be a debilitating force in the workplace. The frustration and anxiety associated with conflict episodes can reduce productivity, lower job satisfaction, and hamper innovation. Conversely, conflict can spur change and adaptation and cement relationships. How people manage their conflict interactions is what makes the difference in creating a positive outcome.

It helps to recognize that conflict is a natural part of organizational life and discard other common misunderstandings about conflict. Knowing what conflict is and is not also helps you develop insights into the process—it involves interdependent people who perceive incompatible goals and interact in order to gain something they value.

Defining conflict seems fairly straightforward—until you begin to consider the numerous factors that help to create and fuel conflict. Individual motives such as the need for consistency, the tendency to mirror behavior, and the need to release psychic energy are compounded by organizational constraints such as specialized roles, ambiguous lines of authority, and scarce resources.

Those who have less trouble coping with conflict have learned to distinguish productive from destructive conflict. Besides looking at how disputants perceived postconflict outcomes, you can identify a number signs of effective conflict management. Remember that constructive conflict interaction is *flexible* rather than rigid and that people avoid repetitive patterns of behavior.

Surviving conflict at work also involves looking at behaviors in context. The specific circumstances surrounding an interaction shape how it develops—what works in one circumstance may not work in another. For this reason, in the next chapters we discuss conflict interaction in different contexts: in one-to-one settings, in group settings, when you are in a position of authority, when you are negotiating or using third parties, and when you must deal with cultural differences. Beginning on the most specific level, in Chapter 2, we focus on how to manage your immediate responses to conflict in one-to-one interactions.

DISCUSSION QUESTIONS

1. How do you usually react to tension caused by conflict? Do you seek consistency?
2. Can you identify indirect aggression in working relationships at your company?
3. Have you recently witnessed any angry outbursts that could possible be indicative of suppressed aggression? How did you manage it?
4. What are some current indicators that there is conflict brewing in your organization?
5. What are some of your more memorable issues of conflict in your organization? How were they handled?
6. Can you identify any additional "myths" about conflict at work in your organization?

EXERCISES

Case Study Revisited

Go back through the case study at the beginning of the chapter. Imagine how events will continue to unfold. How could things have gone differently? What could Gene have done differently? How can Gene and Pat use their conflict episode to make productive changes? What role will Pat's boss need to play? Conversely, how could Gene and Pat's relationship grow into more destructive dimensions?

REFERENCES

Butt, D. (1990, April). *Productive conflict management: A practitioner's perspective.* Paper presented at the Eastern Communication Association Convention, Philadelphia, PA.

Conrad, C. (1985). *Strategic organizational communication: Cultures, situations and adaptation.* New York: Holt, Rinehart & Winston.

Deutsch, M. (1969). Conflicts: Productive and destructive. *The Journal of Social Issues, 25*(1), 7-41.

Deutsch, M. (1973). *The resolution of conflict.* New Haven, CT: Yale University Press.

Festinger, L. (1957). *A theory of cognitive dissonance.* Evanston, IL: Row, Peterson.

Festinger, L. (Ed.). (1964). *Conflict, decision and dissonance.* Stanford, CA: Stanford University Press.

Folger, J.P. & Poole, M.S. (1984). *Working through conflict: A communication perspective.* Glenview, IL: Scott, Foresman.

Frank, A., & Brownell, J. (1989). *Organizational communication and behavior: Communicating to improve performance.* New York: Holt, Rinehart & Winston.

Heider, F. (1946). Attitudes and cognitive organization. *Journal of Psychology, 21,* 107-112.

Hocker, J.L., & Wilmot, W.W. (1985). *Interpersonal conflict.* Dubuque, IA: Wm. C. Brown.

Hocker, J.L., & Wilmot, W.W. (1991). *Interpersonal conflict* (3rd ed.). Dubuque, IA: Wm C. Brown.

Kerr, C. (1964). Industrial conflict and its mediation. *American Journal of Sociology, 60,* 230-245.

Neale, M.A., & Bazerman, M.H. (1991). *Cognition and rationality in negotiation.* New York: The Free Press.

Osgood, C.E., & Tannenbaum, P.H. (1955). The principles of congruity in the prediction of attitude change. *Psychological Review, 62,* 42-55.

Putnam, L.L., & Mumby, D.K. (1992). Organizations, emotion, and the myth of rationality. In S. Fineman (Ed.), *Emotion in organizations* (pp. 36-57). Newbury Park, CA: Sage.

Simons, H.W. (1986). *Persuasion: Understanding, practice and analysis* (3rd ed.). New York: Random House.

▶2

Managing Your Immediate Responses to Conflict

INTRODUCTION

This chapter examines how your personal responses can influence the course of conflict episodes. We focus on how you can manage your own behavior in ways that increase the likelihood of productive outcomes, help you maintain relationships with others, and preserve your mental well-being. Although we realize that you cannot entirely control the conflict process, we discuss ways in which you can control what you say, and how you say it, in order to achieve specific results in one-on-one interactions.

Conflict episodes require that you know what you want to gain from such interactions. We begin this chapter by discussing how to clarify your personal goals and understand the ethical standards of your organization. Realizing what you want helps you decide when confronting conflict is worth the effort involved in taking a stand.

The next section focuses on specific communication skills you can use to manage your own responses to conflicts. We provide specific suggestions on how to maintain cognitive balance, break negative patterns of interaction, and avoid reflexive responses to others. The last section of the chapter deals with strategies for managing the stress associated with conflict, including positive and productive ways of channeling your "psychic energy."

BALANCING PERSONAL ETHICS AND PROFESSIONAL OBLIGATIONS

In conflict situations, you always face decisions about what is "right" and "proper" and "fair." Conflict involves questioning your values as they are challenged by value systems or behaviors that are inconsistent with your own. You will have to make decisions about how to conduct yourself with others, what types of jobs you will perform in life, how you will use your material possessions, what types of power sources you are willing to use, and how you will respond to the use of force by others. You will have to consider how to communicate bad news to your superiors, how to promote your product or service, how to report your business expenses and profits, or how to use your power in dealing with subordinates and superiors. Sometimes, you will have to decide how important conflict issues are to you and determine how far you are willing to go to promote your interpretation of the truth.

Our primary purpose for including a discussion of ethics is to reinforce the need for you to examine your ethical behaviors in relation to the organization. The ethical choices that you make will constrain the conflict-management strategies that you can use. Many of us struggle, as Major Martinez does in the following case, to integrate our personal, professional, and/or life goals with our organizational roles or activities (Eisenberg & Goodall, 1993).

Case Study 2.1: To Tell or Not to Tell

Major Ramone Martinez had just returned from a management workshop on interpersonal skills. Ramone had always felt that he was a "naturally" good listener due to his empathetic nature, but this workshop had sharpened his skills and he was anxious to try them out.

Captain Eileen Davis worked for Ramone in the procurement department of the U.S. Army. She had always had a close professional relationship with him, but lately he seemed more eager to engage her in conversations, during which he would appear to be completely engrossed in whatever she was saying. His new attitude made her feel even closer to him, and with this came an overwhelming desire on Eileen's part to share everything with him. Thus one day she decided to tell him the one secret she had kept from everyone at work—the one thing, in fact, that could mean her job if it became public knowledge. She told Ramone that she was a lesbian. Homosexuals were still not allowed in the military, but she felt that if just one person knew—someone who was her friend and her confidante, even if that person was her supervisor—she would feel much better.

When Eileen told Ramone her secret, he was surprised but, more importantly, suddenly realized that he was now in a precarious position. As her supervisor he had a duty to report her; that was part of the Military Code of Conduct he had sworn to uphold. On the other hand, he had encouraged her frankness by being an active listener, and prompted her to share information with him about herself that a more distanced approach to management surely would not have exposed. In his mind, he was complicit in her situation.*

How should Major Martinez balance his personal ethics with his professional obligations? What would you do? Conflict sometimes prompts an internal struggle, forcing us to chose between our values. This is why it is important to understand your personal and professional priorities.

Clarify Your Personal Goals

Conflict interactions heighten the need to understand your ethical stance. Unethical behavior can cause serious problems, while

---

*Copyright © 1993. From: *Organizational Communication* by Eisenberg & Goodall (p. 244). Reprinted with permission of St. Martin's Press, Inc.

ethical behavior can be very beneficial. The ethical reputation that you establish on the job will influence your conflict interactions. The degree to which someone trusts you will shape the strategies you can utilize for dealing with them.

The struggle over ethics is often associated with difficulty in prioritizing objectives. Values clarification often helps in regaining some perspective on professional priorities. It may also help to fortify your resolve in dealing positively with conflict situations when you have a clear sense that it is really worth it to you to do so—this, in turn, strengthens your commitment to the choices you make. *Knowing how to communicate effectively is only as good as the willingness to actually do so*, and willingness is related to understanding your priorities.

A basic assessment of your value system and its impact on your professional priorities clarifies the foundation against which you gauge your actions—it dictates what behaviors in which you will, or will not, engage. Having some clear insights into "what makes you tick" helps you make better assessments of what you feel comfortable with, both in terms of your sense of "right" and "wrong" and of your own personal style. This kind of assessment provides you with your own personal baseline from which to explore the options, or choices for action that are available to you in any given situation.

Many of the conflicts we have with people close to us involve values—a basic difference in likes and dislikes. We have included an exercise at the end of this chapter that can help you assess your professional priorities. A basic inventory of your value system and its impact on your professional priorities clarifies the foundation for your behaviors. We have included an exercise at the end of the chapter adapted from Simon (1978), "The Miracle Worker." It is designed to help you get in touch with what is important to you.

Know the Standards of Your Organization

Andrews and Baird (1992) pointed out that organizations must also make decisions about what's fair and not fair in dealing with employees and customers, products and services, social systems and the environment. They referred to how Bowen H. McCoy, Managing Director of Morgan Stanley & Co., Investment Bankers, defined ethics in the context of modern organizations: "Ethics involves the art of integration and compromise, not blind obedience and conformity. . . . Ethics deals with free choice among alternatives" (p. 89).

Besides clarifying your personal priorities, you also need to understand how your company's policies translate into day-to-day practices. Many corporations now have formal policies that dictate ethical standards for dealing with coworkers, superiors, subordinates, customers, and suppliers. Does your company's policy prohibiting accepting gifts from outside contractors mean that you should split the $75 lunch tab with the sales representative who suggested the expensive restaurant in the first place? Should a sports reporter also participate in evaluating the worth of players by voting on who belongs in the Hall of Fame? Do these instances represent a conflict of interest? You need to know how your company's ethical standards translate into actual applications for your daily business interactions.

Ethics is not simply a matter of knowing organizational rules and obeying the law. Ethical decisions range from simple convictions such as "I will not steal," to complex assessments of the means and ends, the needs of the few versus the needs of the many, and immediate to long-term consequences of choices. Solomon (1990) pointed out that ethics is a way of life, not abstract premises unconnected to actions. "It is the awareness that one is an intrinsic part of a social order, in which the interests of others and one's own interests are inevitably intertwined" (p. 5).

An important part of managing conflict is understanding how to balance your personal priorities with your professional obligations. Although each specific instance involves different elements in the juggling process, we suggest that you consider the following questions:

- What's most important to me in the long term?
- W hat am I willing to put on the line?
- What actions will allow me to sleep at night?
- What actions will allow me to be effective in my job?

Before you can chose a conflict strategy, you have to be clear about your personal ethics and your professional obligations.

TAKING A STAND

Clarifying your priorities will help you decide when confronting conflict is worth the time and effort. It is not enough that you "know you are right"—your voice must be heard if you wish to have your views carry some weight and maintain the respect of your colleagues. Similarly, Putnam and Wilson (1982) found that managers who confronted, rather than avoided, problems were more respected by employees. Managers who avoided conflicts were perceived by employees as not doing their jobs because they were not working to solve organizational problems.

Deciding Whether to Confront

When deciding whether or not to precipitate conflicts, you should consider a number of factors (Donohue & Kolt, 1992). First, you should ask, "How important is the issue?" (p. 27). If you feel the issue is significant, and other people in your organization feel similarly, then confrontation is probably more appropriate than avoidance.

However, the issue's significance must be weighed against an assessment of the strength of the relationships among the disputants. A second question to ask is, "How committed are people to maintaining their relationships? If the relationships are strong, confrontation can help to clarify issues and emotions. If, on the other hand, people are not committed to each other, confrontation might give them the opportunity to destroy the relationships. You have to balance the importance of the issue against the potential costs to the relationships that can result from a keener, more vivid awareness of differences.

Confrontation also takes time. Time demands convey a competitive message that undercuts people's willingness to work cooperatively. Thus, a third question to ask is, "How much time is available?" If time is limited, then avoidance is probably appropriate (unless this becomes a consistent pattern).

Another factor to assess is the organizational climate. Work groups develop unspoken rules about how conflict should be handled. A fourth question to ask when deciding whether to avoid or confront is, "What's the level of interpersonal skills within the group?" If people are defensive rather than supportive, confrontation is not likely to be constructive.

In addition, the individuals involved must be willing and able to adapt their work habits—you should thus ask, "How flexible is this person?" Finally, you need to consider issues of physical safety. "If you expect personal harm," Donohue and Kolt (1992) wrote, "then avoidance is mandatory" (p. 33).

Raising Delicate Issues

Making changes to resolve incompatibilities is a difficult challenge for most people, even when it involves something positive. You can take several steps to minimize the potential for hostility and overcome resistance to change. Carefully preparing for the interaction is particularly important when raising delicate issues. Before you say anything, you should take the following steps (Adler, 1992):

1. Identify what you hope to accomplish in the interaction. Have a clear idea of what you want to have happen after you have spoken up. Do you want to express your feelings to "clear the air" and refocus a working relationship, or are you attempting to persuade the other person to support your viewpoints? Perhaps you need to direct a change in the other person's behavior. Asking for change depends on establishing just cause—you must establish a good reason for them to put forth the effort and lay out specific objectives to be accomplished as a result of the change. You may need to point out the dissatisfying aspects of the current situation or clarify the "payoffs" in doing things differently. Different goals will require different approaches.

2. Choose the best time to speak up. Timing is important in getting results. Try to gauge the work flow and select a time when the office stress levels are not at their highest. Take whatever steps you can to insure that the person feels sufficiently secure about the situation. Don't introduce change as a surprise!

3. Rehearse what you're going to say. Preparing your thoughts in advance will help you make your point quickly and prevent you from blurting out an angry statement you'll regret later. Think about your general ideas and, perhaps, a few key phrases you'll use to make your ideas clear. This helps you to clarify your focus . . . *you are not scripting your message.* Remember, planning for a conversation to go a certain way does not insure that's how it will actually go! Having the points that you want to make clear in your mind will help you get your ideas across in the course of the conversation.

When the time comes to deliver your message, follow these guidelines:

1. Pinpoint the specific behavior you want to discuss. The best descriptions are specific and objective. Avoid accusations or mind reading regarding the other person's motives.

WRONG   "Your work is sloppy."
RIGHT   "The last three status reports have been
             a week or more late and you haven't
             compared actual payroll hours to budget
             projections."

2. *Explain your reaction to the behavior.* Your explanation should include your interpretation of the behavior and your feelings about the action.

WRONG   "You're not paying attention to details."
RIGHT   "I'm disappointed because I can't give the
             home office specifics when they ask how
             the project is progressing."

3. *Make a request.* The best requests are specific and limited to one or two changes at a time. They also ask for responses that are within the ability of the other person to give.

WRONG   "Try to be more punctual and complete
             from now on."
RIGHT   "I'd like your promise that your reports will
             include payroll hours and be ready on
             Mondays from now on."

4. *Describe the consequences.* The consequence statement should discuss the payoffs (both for you and the other person) of reaching accord. These payoffs can be tangible (money, time) and intangible (psychological comfort, friendship).

WRONG   "You'd better speed up before it's too late!
RIGHT   "If the status reports are complete and on
             time, neither of us will have to duck calls
             from the home office."

DEVELOPING COMMUNICATION SKILLS TO HANDLE UNEXPECTED CONFLICTS

Although it's nice to have the luxury of time to organize our thoughts, many conflicts on the job catch us when we are least expecting them. We don't have an opportunity to plan our strategies and focus our priorities. What can you do in such cases? Developing some basic communication skills will help.

In the following case study, notice how poor listening and defensive reactions made it difficult for the Human Resources Manager and the Client Services Supervisor to understand each other. Because these disputants did not "double check" their understanding of what the "other" was saying, their interaction exaggerated the differences between them, leading them to over-look areas in which they had common opinions.

Case Study 2.2: Head Office Policies versus Immediate Priorities

Susan Wood was Human Resources manager for a local unem-ployment office in Erie, Pennsylvania. Most of the Unemployment Commission's policies and procedures were established by the head office in Harrisburg and announced to the local offices through regional offices. Although regional managers were fre-quently consulted about new procedures, local office managers sel-dom had input. Local Human Resource Managers were typically informed of policy changes through memos from their Regional Managers.

Recently, Susan had been bothered by a policy memo which mandated that 80% of all full-time employees hired during any six-month period had to be women or people of color. "This will make it hard for us to hire during the rest of the winter," Susan thought. In the last two months, the only people hired in the local office were two white males, and there were four more months to go in this reporting period. To meet these new requirements, only minority candidates could be hired during the next four months, which were likely to be very busy with seasonal layoffs occurring. "This is typical," Susan thought.

One morning, as Susan was reading her mail, Chuck Saunders, the local office Client Services Director, walked into her office. "Susan, I've got a problem, and I need some help from you," Chuck began.

"What's up?" asked Susan. "I'll sure do what I can."

"It's about Bill Sweet," Chuck continued. "He wants to return after taking a try at the insurance business for a few months. He was one of our best Client Service Coordinators, but your secretary tells me we can't reinstate him because he's not a minority. What can we do about this? We certainly ought to rein-state Bill. We're way short of people, and he can do three times the work that an inexperienced person could do."

"Well," replied Susan, "the minority hiring procedures apply to newly hired employees, and that's what Bill would be. He was

terminated, not put on leave. According to the procedures, there's no way we can hire him until four months from now."

Chuck's eyes widened and he began to gesture to emphasize his points: "I can't believe it! I really need someone to help cut the case backlog in my department, and you're saying we have to add to our workload by bringing in new people to train. You're being unreasonable. Sure we could use Bill in four months, but he'll never wait that long for the job. He has other opportunities right now."

"Well," said Susan, "It's dangerous to make exceptions to head-office procedures. You know what happens when you start making exceptions. If I let you hire Bill, I'll have all the other department heads in here saying, 'Hire this guy.' You're not the one who has to explain why our office didn't meet the goals. We might not make the 80% mark even if we hire all minorities for the next four months. Don't yell at me. I didn't make the policy. If you want to change it . . ."

"Susan," Chuck interrupted, "I need help in my department now. You aren't going to get fired for being off a few percentage points in your affirmative action numbers."

"Do you have a problem with minorities?" Susan countered. We're an unemployment office. If we won't hire minorities, how can we expect other employers to hire all the minority clients we're trying to place? As I tried to say before, if you want to suggest a change, see the Regional Office Director."

"Come on, Susan, this isn't the problem." Chuck blurted, his voice rising in volume as he continued. "I need someone, and there's a really competent person available. My people are starting to lean on me about getting some help to spread the case load. We have an especially bad backlog on our hands right now with all the Corning layoffs, and you're not being any help at all."

"Well, you got yourself into this jam," replied Susan. "If you were bringing some lower level employees along by running a good training program for them, you wouldn't get caught short. You'd have a person all ready to step into a coordinator's job whenever you needed someone."

"I need a coordinator right now," Chuck snapped, "and you refuse to help me out! This is ridiculous," he said as he stamped out of the office. (This case study was adapted from Fisher, 1981).

Avoid Sending Defensive Messages

Neither Susan nor Chuck effectively managed their responses toward each other in this interaction. Each became defensive, protecting their egos rather than clarifying their objectives and listening to what the other had to say. Their interaction illustrates the importance of avoiding defending yourself at the expense of the "other." It is very easy to become defensive when someone comes at you with an urgent problem or complaint. However, defensive communication is rarely effective. It doesn't clarify what the problem is, but it does damage relationships and lead to endless cycles of face saving.

Gibb (1961) identified the differences between supportive and defensive communication patterns. *Descriptive* comments are predominant in supportive communication, whereas *evaluative* statements are the norm in defensive interaction. Descriptive language focuses on observations rather than on inferences, reporting what occurred without offering a judgment. Judgment refers to an evaluation of good or bad, nice or otherwise.

Descriptive	Evaluative
"Your analysis omitted three important facts and your recommendation was hidden in text."	"That was the worst, sloppiest, most incomplete analysis I've ever seen.

Problem orientation, rather than attempted *control*, is another particularly important facet of supportive communication. Problem orientation asks the "other" to join in a mutual process of problem solving. A controlling orientation focuses on forcing or fooling the other person into complying. The manager who smiles at every complaint regardless of its merit or ability to be addressed and says, "Yes, that is a legitimate problem, I'll get on it" will create a defensive climate because sooner or later it will become apparent that this is just a strategy to silence the complaining employee. No one likes to be manipulated and controlled.

Problem-Oriented	Control-Oriented
"Let's discuss your transportation situation. How do you get to work?	"Don't be late again."

Supportive communication implies a relationship of *equality*, whereas evaluative, controlling comments indicate a relationship based on *superiority*.

Equality	Superiority
"I'd like to hear your ideas."	"I've been there and know more."

Supportive communication relies on pronouns such as "us" and "we," whereas defensive communication highlights the distinctions between "you" and "me."

Defensive comments are also *neutral*, featuring impersonal rules and procedures applied regardless of the circumstances. Failing to recognize legitimate individual needs can heighten conflict. Supportive communication, on the other hand, is characterized by *empathy*.

Empathetic	Neutral
"I can understand why you are upset about this performance appraisal."	"Everyone reacts to their performance appraisals."

If we treat others as important, significant parts of the organization and acknowledge their individual contributions, we are fostering a supportive climate in which people feel they are not just another number in the organization.

Finally, the last contrast Gibb (1961) identified, *certainty* versus *provisionalism*, deals with the degree to which communication is marked by the attitude, "I have all the answers." In a climate of certainty, there is little to be accomplished through communication because the dogmatic approach leaves no room for counter interpretations. If you know everything, what is the point in talking? A provisional style, on the other hand, qualifies interpretations, conveying the sense that: "I don't have all the answers, but perhaps we could try this." A provisional style acknowledges change and labels interpretations as tentative rather than as absolute.

Provisional	Certain
"I think that LIFO accounting has some advantages in this case."	"LIFO is the way to go."

Cross (1978) provided a clear, succinct summary of how to overcome defensive communications. He pointed out that "simply recognizing that defensive communication is debilitating to interpersonal relationships, and that it exists to some degree in all organizations, is not enough" (p. 441). Cross emphasized that individuals need to know how to apply effective antidotes to the defensive communication so often associated with conflict:

1. *Keep your responses descriptive—don't be judgmental.* Focus on facts and behaviors rather than on personality characteristics. Attacking, evaluative statements are often called "you" language because they point a verbal finger of accusation at the receiver: "You're saying we have to have to add to our workload" or "You're being unreasonable." By contrast, descriptive language is termed "I" language because it focuses on the speaker instead of judging the other person. "I'm frustrated at not being able to make use of a good employee." When using "I" messages, you assume responsibility for your own feelings rather than projecting them onto the "other." These direct expressions are a valuable tool in setting a positive tone for the interaction.

<u>"You" language:</u>	"You are irresponsible in being chronically late."
<u>"I" language:</u>	"I've counted five times this month that you have been late. I've had to make a lot of excuses when the boss asks about you. I'm tired of making excuses, and I hope you'll start showing up on time."

Chuck's "you" statements to Susan presented his judgments about her. They did not help either person identify the real issues of difference; instead, evaluative statements prompted Susan to harden her position about the rules and return fire with her own "you" statements: "Do you have a problem with minorities?" As each person defended themselves, creative solutions to the problem were overlooked. No one thought to suggest hiring Bill as a temporary worker or part-time consultant; instead, defensive communication led to trading insults.

2. *Appeal to a common goal, don't exercise control.* Indicate areas of agreement and reinforce where mutual efforts are important in the continuation of your working relationship. Identifying

agreements underscores the desirability of resolving differences and realizing the common good. Efforts at exercising control largely defeats the purpose of effective listening and may serve as fuel for the fire in a combative or hostile interaction. Chuck, for example, tries to control Susan by saying: "They aren't going to fire you for being a few percentage points off." Susan responds in kind by telling Chuck to see the Regional Director. Their common attitudes about head office procedures got lost in their efforts to control each other's behavior.

3. *Respond to people, don't react.* The old adage "think before you speak" is a good one to follow when dealing with direct confrontations. Reacting to other people leaves you vulnerable to manipulation. Unthinking, gut-level reactions leave you at the mercy of someone who may simply enjoy goading you into saying and doing things that are not in your best interest. Susan reacted to Chuck rather than responded to him. By controlling your responses, you can allow room for the other person to "save face" as well.

We are not implying here that you should pretend not to be angry or displeased with what is being said or done, nor are we suggesting that you should deny how you feel about what is happening. Our intention here is to illustrate the importance of choosing responses that allow you to achieve your objectives for the interaction.

Learning how to respond effectively also involves being congruent in your responses—match your intentions to what you say and how you say it. A large part of the communication process involves nonverbal messages. Your tone and physical stance (including gestures and facial expressions) should send the same signal as the meaning of your words.

Using descriptive language, focusing on common interests, and controlling your gut-level reactions are helpful for creating and maintaining a supportive atmosphere for dealing with conflict. Deciding on an effective response in a given situation also depends on your ability to identify the source, or sources, of problems. Responding effectively to conflict depends, to a large extent, on *how well you can listen* to the other person to find out how they perceive the situation. Listening is a skill that must be learned and learned well, and it does not come easily. It is particularly difficult when you are coming under fire from a hostile colleague.

Listen to the "Other"

Effective listening requires overcoming the tendency to think about what you're going to say next while the other person is talking. Rather than formulating the argument or criticism to "return fire" as soon as they stop to take a breath, strive to focus on the source of the conflict. Here are several ways in which you can identify the nature of the difficulty as you listen:

1. *Focus on what is being said rather than how you feel about it.* Listen for the details of the problem in terms of concrete actions or behaviors. As you many recall from chapter 1, it is important to concentrate on what is being said or done rather than on the "personalities" involved. Focusing on behaviors allows you to concentrate on tangible actions rather than on intangible personality traits. Actions can be changed more easily than personalities.

- tangible action focus: "It's hard for me to listen to you when you raise your voice and pound on the table."
- intangible personality focus: "You are a wild animal when you are angry!"

2. *Focus on observations rather than inferences.* Observations refer to what we can see or hear in the behavior of another person, whereas inferences refer to interpretations and conclusions we make about what we see or hear.

- observation: "You look very upset."
- inference: "I know you hate me."

3. *Focus on the "here and now."* Strive to avoid "injustice gathering" as you listen. Deal with the immediacy of THIS inter-action and keep your attention and reactions on the issue at hand, not on past history and the distortions that come with the passing of time.

- here-and-now: "I submitted the EPA test results before the deadline."
- injustice gathering: "This is the fourth time this month you've tried to pin something on me."

4. *Focus on WHAT is said rather then WHY it is said.* By focusing on what is said, it is easier to "get the facts." Listen for the what, how, when, and where of what is said. The "why" takes you from the observable to the inferred, and brings up questions of "motive" or "intent." Clarify the issue first—ferreting out hidden agendas can be treacherous and is rarely successful if someone harbors truly malicious intentions against you.

Clarify Perceptions

Effective listening is not simply a matter of silently following along as the other person speaks. It also entails asking questions and "double checking" your understanding of what the person is saying. There are three basic techniques for clarifying meaning and enhancing understanding:

1. *Paraphrasing* tells the speaker what the message means to you. The goal is to communicate, in your own style, what you heard the person say. Phrases such as "I hear you saying that . . ." or "In other words . . ." typically precede paraphrasing comments. Paraphrasing is not the same as parroting the speaker's words. By using your own words to express the speaker's message, you attempt to assure accurate understanding and confirm the speaker's need to be heard. Leave time for the speaker to respond to your paraphrasing. The following exchange illustrates how effective paraphrasing can help get to the root of the problem:

Gretchen:	We have a real problem here. The copy room will be closed and Weiss needs the Clover account materials today.
Howard	(paraphrasing): Now let me get this straight. You need me to have the copies made right away and the packet delivered to Mr. Weiss's office by one o'clock today.
Gretchen:	The copies need to be made before lunch because the machine will be serviced, but you don't need to deliver the packet to Weiss until five o'clock.

By paraphrasing, Howard clarified actual time deadlines rather than relying on generalities.

2. *Perception checking* involves describing in a tentative fashion what you perceive as the other's point of view or state of mind.

Coworker Mary:	(annoyed) This is a lot of production notes you have for me to go over.
Coworker Mel:	(checking Mary's perceptions) I get the feeling you've been swamped with work today.

By articulating the feelings he sensed, Mel provided Mary with the opportunity to agree or disagree. Don't trust your perceptions without testing them by reflecting them back to the other party.

3. *Asking for clarification* shows you are interested and want to understand what the other person is saying. The goal is to unearth new information rather than review what has already been said.

Richard:	This proposal is not what I asked for at all.
Bob:	(asking for clarification) Nothing about the proposal is acceptable?
Richard:	There are some attractive aspects, but parts of it do not seem feasible.
Bob:	Which parts specifically do not seem feasible?

Asking other people to clarify their meaning is an underutilized communication skill.

Clarifying the perceptions of others is often a critical factor in responding to conflict. People have a tendency to hear what they want, or expect, to hear. It is important to double check your own perceptions of where the other person is coming from. You may also need to take extra steps to help insure that the person to whom you are speaking is getting the meaning you intended. Susan, for example, might have reflected the feelings she observed in Chuck and tried to clarify their source: "You look frustrated. Is it the procedures or your work load?"

Comedy routines have been built around the conflict that stems from people failing to clarify perceptions. Most people have a hard time finding humor in a situation when they are frustrated by the consequences of "miscommunicating." Although clarifying perceptions can be difficult, it is usually worth the effort even if the conversation ends in an exasperated, "Well, why didn't you say that in the first place!"

Developing effective communication skills is a critical factor in increasing personal control and focus. These skills need to be combined, however, with a repertoire of personal coping strategies to meet the demands associated with dealing regularly with high conflict/high stress situations. In the next section, we turn our attention to strategies for coping with the stress created by conflict.

COPING WITH THE STRESS OF CONFLICT

The strategies for positive conflict management are essentially based on two premises: (a) the parties involved in the conflict are willing to attempt to resolve it, and (b) the parties involved will be trustworthy and not abusive to one another. What happens when this is not the case? When you must bare the brunt of other people's behavior? When you find yourself asking, "Why am I always the one who has to 'deal' with the situation?" or feeling as though you're "tired of having to do all of the work to keep things running smoothly around here!"

When conflict and stress take on a snowball effect, the result is what is commonly referred to as *burnout*. Maslach and Jackson (1981) defined burnout as a physiological and psychological state characterized by emotional exhaustion, depersonalization, and lack of on-the-job accomplishment. Although many of the factors associated with conflict may, to a large extent, be beyond your control, your personal response to the situation is your choice. How you make that choice depends on a wide variety of factors—your ethical stance, your individual communication skills, your personal style, who's involved in the interaction, the context in which the situation is unfolding, and how you feel that day. Identifying what you cherish, what type of person you want to be, and how you want to be regarded by others as well as coming to grips with what you are willing to put up with or not is one step in coping with stress whether it stems directly from conflict situations or not.

Monitor Your Personal Stress

Enhancing your level of satisfaction in dealing with conflict situations ultimately involves monitoring your personal stress levels. Although a rare individual may indicate that he or she "thrives" on facing challenges, enjoys verbal sparring, or even looks forward to facing confrontations, experience generally shows that most people do not. Irritability, fatigue, depression, or being "stressed out" increases the likelihood of defensive communication. The possibility of moving into a conflict situation that may otherwise have been avoided also increases. Having a clearer understanding of your own stress tolerance is a helpful tool in coping with stress and its counterproductive outcomes.

Not all stress is bad; in fact, some stress is essential to living a full, productive life (Selye, 1974). Given the high-stress atmosphere of today's work environment, measuring stress levels may be critical to daily performance. A self-scoring stress test can help identify problem areas. The American Institute of Stress developed the following short quiz to help you estimate how well you handle stress on the job (see Table 2.1).

TABLE 2.1. HOW MUCH JOB STRESS DO YOU HAVE?

Enter a number from the scale below that best describes you and your reactions.

Strongly Disagree	Agree Somewhat	Strongly Agree
1 2 3	4 5 6	7 8 9 10

1. I can't honestly say what I really think or get things of my chest at work. _____
2. My job has a lot responsibility, but I don't have very much authority. _____
3. I could usually do a much better job if I were given more time.
4. I seldom receive adequate acknowledgment or appreciation when my work is really good. _____
5. In general, I'm not particularly proud of or satisfied with my job. _____
6. I have the impression I am repeatedly picked on or discriminated against at work. _____
7. My workplace environment is not very pleasant or particularly safe. _____
8. My job often interferes with my family and social obligations or personal needs. _____
9. I tend to have frequent arguments with superiors, coworkers, or customers. _____
10. Most of the time I feel that I have very little control over my life at work. _____

Add up the replies to each question for your Total Job Stress Score _____

A score of 10-30 means you handle stress on your job well; 40-60, moderately well; 70-100, you're encountering problems that need to be resolved.

A number of different stress tests have been developed according to occupation. Additional self-scoring stress tests are usually available through a company's human resource or personnel departments or the company psychologist. Data from a stress test combined with *daily observations* can help you identify your personal stress patterns. Monitoring also helps you to recognize when you need a cooling-off period, when you need to reschedule various activities to better regulate stress, and when you need to avoid certain people or situations.

Develop Personalized Coping Strategies

Coping with stress, like experiencing it, is highly individualized. Martinez (1989) identified six general guidelines for coping positively with stress:

1. *Find some "wiggle room."* Focus on what can be done rather than what can't. Individuals may feel handicapped by external constraints—regulations, working conditions, and limitations on resources and time. Combs (cited in Frymier, 1987) suggests, "There is always room to wiggle. There is always at least a little room to experiment, to try to change things" (p. 12). If you do not have the resources or authorization to implement an ideal solution or completely address a situation, exercise what is within your control.

2. *Cycle intensity.* Plan your work schedule so that you can balance periods of intense work or high pressure with less demanding activities. This type of planning, or cycling, allows regeneration and/or recovery periods rather than a never-ending, uphill battle.

3. *Balance high-stress with low-stress activities.* The old adage about not bringing your office problems home with you reflects the need for balance between stress and relaxation. High stress should be consistently matched with low stress or relaxation. The idea is to regularly insure for balance rather than to collapse. Enforced rest can, in and of itself, be a source of high stress!

4. *Learn to relax under stress as well as times of rest.* It is important to develop methods of physically and emotionally relaxing while under stress. Whether it involves 10 quiet minutes in your office with the door closed practicing transcendental meditation or playing "Tetrus," it is important to be able to take a brief time out when under high stress. Relaxing, even briefly, will

help you slow down the emotional reactions and, when you return to the problem, begin thinking about a solution.

5. *Change distress to eustress.* According to Selye (1974), "It is not stress but our reaction to stress that creates problems physically and psychologically. A negative reaction results in distress—a physical and psychological state tied to high blood pressure, ulcers, backaches, and headaches. A positive reaction results in eustress—a motivating force that heightens energy levels and increases productivity" (p. 280).

6. *Exercise regularly.* Generally, the person who exercises regularly is better able to meet the demands stress places on the body and to maintain emotional as well as physical equilibrium in stressful situations.

Colleagues and mentors are especially helpful for sharing common concerns, relating various experiences, benefiting from each others' trials and errors, and providing a safe avenue for venting frustrations and hostilities. Support systems may also lead to low-stress activities and recreation that help you balance high stress on the job. Developing a solid support system may begin by simply generating "who do you know" lists and may be as complex as developing sophisticated analyses of networking and coalition building.

In addition to developing specific response strategies, Holt, Fine, and Tollefson (1987) indicated that it is important to cultivate what they refer to as "stress hardiness." They mention three overall factors that seem to contribute to stress hardiness: (a) commitment—"the tendency to be involved in (rather than alienated from) many aspects of one's life"; (b) challenge—"the belief that change, rather than stability, is characteristic of life"; and (c) control—believing and acting "as if one is influential (rather than helpless) in the course of events in one's life" (pp. 51-52). They emphasized that "If you are involved and committed, you are more likely to find meaning and value in who you are and what you do, despite the stress involved in your job" (p. 56).

Coping with the stress generated by conflict is obviously part of a larger stress-management approach. Keeping stress under control is helpful in avoiding some types of conflict as well as "scaling down" the potential magnitude of conflict interactions. Clear-headed, healthy people are generally better at handling conflict.

SUMMARY

Although you cannot control what other people will say and do, you can take certain steps to help make your interactions more productive—the specific behaviors you use will influence how conflict interactions will play out. Getting in touch with your basic ideals gives you insights into how you deal with other people. Clarifying your personal goals and the professional standards of your organization may help you decide when taking a stand is worth the potential costs.

Managing your immediate responses involves careful listening, maintaining a sharp focus on specific objectives, and clarifying meanings as you go along. Avoiding defensive communication plays a key role in keeping interactions productive as well. Being problem-oriented, open-minded, and respectful of others is critical. Your ability to carefully raise delicate issues is important in motivating others to change problematic behaviors or adopt new behaviors.

Conflict is clearly associated with physical and emotional stress. How well you are able to cope with the stress associated with conflict depends on your attitude, outlook, and expectations. Monitoring your personal stress levels can help you identify conflict "hot spots." Stress reduction and successful conflict management often go hand in hand; by developing personalized coping strategies, you arm yourself to deal more productively with conflict interactions.

DISCUSSION QUESTIONS

1. Can you identify any unethical behavior in your organization? How could ethical behavior be reinforced in your organization?
2. What are some of the professional standards that shape behavior in your workplace?
3. Do you perceive yourself to be an effective listener? Why or why not?
4. Think of a problem that you are having with a current coworker, subordinate, or superior. Identify the specific problem behavior that you would like to discuss. How would you describe this behavior to the other person without prompting a defensive response?

5. Based on the way you manage stress, which personalized coping strategies do you think work best for you?
6. Do you have a support system in your organization? If not, how could you build one?

EXERCISES

Testing What You Value (adapted from Sidney B. Simon: *Values Clarification: A Handbook of Practical Strategies for Students & Teachers.* Values Associates, Hadley, MA, 1978. Reprinted with permission from author.)

Purpose

To help you get in touch with your feelings about what is important to you by confronting many attractive alternatives.

Procedure

Step One. Read the character descriptions for the 15 "miracle workers" listed below. Select the 5 miracle workers you value the highest—the five whose gifts you would most like to receive. Rank them 1 (most valued) through 5.

After you have selected your top five, go back through the list and select 5 more names to establish your top 10. Rank these 6 through 10. This leaves 5 miracle workers in the least desirable group.

_____ Dr. Dorian Grey—A noted plastic surgeon. He can make you look exactly as you want to look by means of a new painless technique. Your ideal physical appearance can be a reality.

_____ Mark I. Table—A job placement expert. The job or career of your choice, in the location of your choice, will be yours!

_____ Jedediah Methuselah—Guarantees you long life (to the age of 200), with your aging process slowed down proportionately. For example, at the age of 60 you will look and feel like you are 20.

_____ Dr. Ruth B. Good—Expert in the area of sexual relations who guarantees that you will be the perfect male or female, will enjoy sex, and will bring pleasure to others.

_____ Dr. Yin Yang—An organismic expert. He will provide you with perfect health and protection from physical injury throughout your life.

_____ Dr. Knot Not Ginott—An expert in dealing with bosses. She guarantees that you will never have any problems with your superiors again. They will accept your values and your behavior. You will be free from control and badgering.

_____ Ann Archist—An expert on authority. She will ensure that you are never again bothered by authorities. Her services will make you immune to all control that you consider unfair by your company, the police, and the government.

_____ "Pop" Larity—He guarantees that you will have the friends you want now and in the future. You will find it easy to approach those you like and they will find you easily approachable.

_____ Dr. Maxine Smart—She will develop your common sense and your intelligence to a level in excess of 150 IQ. It will remain at this level through your entire lifetime.

_____ Rocky Fellah—Wealth will be yours, with guaranteed schemes for earning millions within weeks.

_____ Dwight D. DeGawl—This world-famous leadership expert will train you quickly. You will be listened to, looked up to, and respected by those around you.

_____ Dr. Leo B. Valentine—You will be well-liked by all and will never be lonely. A life filled with love will be yours.

_____ Dr. Claire Voyant—All of your questions about the future will be answered, continually, through the training of this soothsayer.

_____ Dr. Hinnah Self—Guarantees that you will have self-knowledge, self-liking, self-respect, and self-confidence. True self-assurance will be yours.

_____ Prof. Val U Clear—With her help, you will always know what you want, and you will be completely clear on any muddy issues.

Step Two. Try to identify any patterns in your choices. What seems to link the five most desirable people and what joins the five least desirable to you? What values were you upholding in your choices? Are there any choices that somehow seem out of place with the others in that grouping?

Step Three. Make a list of things you can do to achieve what your top five miracle workers could do for you. What "miracles" do you want to strive for? How can you help yourself accomplish them?

REFERENCES

Adler, R.B. (1992). *Communicating at work: Principles and practices for business and the professions.* New York: McGraw-Hill.

Andrews, P.H., & Baird, J.E. (1992). *Communication for business and the professions* (5th ed.). Dubuque, IA: Wm. C. Brown.

Cross, G.P. (1978). How to overcome defensive communications. *Personnel Journal,* August, 441-443.

Donohue, W.A., & Kolt, R. (1992). Managing interpersonal conflict. Newbury Park: Sage.

Eisenberg, E.M., & Goodall, H.L. (1993). *Organizational communication: Balancing creativity and constraint.* New York: St. Martin's Press.

Fisher, D. (1981). A situation for diagnosis. In *Communication in organizations* (pp. 27-28). New York: West.

Frymier, J. (1987). Bureaucracy and the neutering of teachers. *Phi Delta Kappan, 69*(1), 9-16.

Gibb, J. (1961). Defensive communication. *Journal of Communication, 11,* 141-148.

Holt, P., Fine, M.J., & Tollefson, N. (1987). Mediating stress: Survival of the hardy. *Psychology in the Schools, 24,* 51-58.

Martinez, J.G. (1989). Cooling off before burning out. *Academic Therapy, 24*(3), 9-16.

Maslach, C., & Jackson, S.E. (1981). The measure of experienced burnout. *Journal of Occupational Behavior, 2,* 99-113.

Putnam, L.L., & Wilson, C.E. (1982). Communicative strategies in organizational conflicts: Reliability and validity of a measurement scale. In M. Burgoon (Ed.), *Communication Yearbook 6* (pp. 629-652). Beverly Hills, CA: Sage.

Selye, H. (1974). *Stress without distress.* New York: New American Library.

Simon, S.B. (1978). *Values classifications: A handbook of practical strategies for teachers and students.* Sunderland, MA: Values Press.

Solomon, M. (1990). *Working with difficult people.* Englewood Cliffs, NJ: Prentice-Hall.

▶ 3

Dealing with Conflict in Work Teams

INTRODUCTION

In chapter 2, we examined conflict in terms of one-to-one interaction. In this chapter, we shift our attention to considering conflict processes in group settings and focus on productive actions you can take as a member of a work team. Effective teams require responsible, committed members who help the group function productively. Even if you are not the designated leader of a project team or the manager of a work unit, you can understand the factors that shape group interaction and develop communication skills that facilitate effective problem solving and coordination.

To begin, we explain the importance of managing conflict between you and your coworkers and identify the characteristics of effective and ineffective teams. Because the context surrounding conflict episodes influences interaction, we describe how you can identify and influence the important features of your workplace climate. Next, we suggest ways in which you can help a work team clarify goals and manage hidden agendas, and we highlight the important roles that must be performed to facilitate decision making and maintain group cohesion. We conclude by considering how to handle conflict as it erupts in meetings because of problem participants who refuse to coordinate their individual goals with group objectives.

RECOGNIZING THE TRAITS OF EFFECTIVE WORK TEAMS?

It is a simple fact of organizational life that you must often coordinate your efforts with those of your coworkers within and outside of your functional area. Team management is increasingly popular as organizations attempt to "restructure" the traditional hierarchy to eliminate redundant levels of middle managers, improve internal coordination, and speed response time to market fluctuations. The concept of self-directed work teams who report directly to the chief executive is alluring. Given control of their own fates, team management advocates assert, employees will be more motivated, work faster, and keep an eye on the bottom line.

The reality of team management is not quite so rosy. As management consultant Douglas K. Smith explained: "A completely diverse group must agree on a goal, put the notion of individual accountability aside and figure out how to work with each other" (cited in Stern, 1993, p. F5). Turf battles can erupt as workers feel conflicting loyalties brought about by their memberships in multiple "teams". Communication across functional areas can be difficult because members operate from unique, unshared points of view. When the Dow Chemical Company used a team approach to develop a new product, conflict emerged between research and development people who wanted to cautiously build a prototype and "volume-driven manufacturing managers [who] preferred a slight variation on an existing product and a quick start up of mass production" (Stern, 1993, p. F5).

Managers accustomed to traditional hierarchies can be threatened by the concept of "empowered" subordinates who might come to different solutions to workplace problems. Status struggles can be a constant source of conflict. Teams that report to more than one manager can find it takes longer to accomplish a task than it did before team management. Finally, top management must consistently support team management, adapting a number of organizational practices. While attempting to "empower" workers in their management training, IBM simultaneously instituted a performance-appraisal ranking system in which all units were rank ordered in relation to others. Individuals within functional areas were similarly rank ordered. The ranking system undercut the organization's training on team building, sending conflicting signals to employees.

In order for teams to be effective, top management must make a commitment to reworking their organization and employees must learn how to deal with their differences, coordinating their efforts among themselves rather than kicking all problems upstairs for "the boss" to decide. The trend toward team management places a premium on your ability to successfully manage conflict between you and your coworkers.

We use the term *team* to apply to any organizational element whose members have a common task, interact regularly, and report to a common supervisor. For example, the element might be a department within a functional area, a project team working on a new product, or a staff group. The team may include people from several levels in the organization, but they have some common task or tasks to perform and share a common fate in reporting to a common supervisor.

What, then, does an effective work team look like? Table 3.1 summarizes six characteristics of effective teams and contrasts the traits of ineffective teams. Despite the many nuances that make each group unique, effective teams share a number of common traits. They have clear goals that are cooperatively structured; leadership functions are shared by team members, and decision-making procedures are adapted to accommodate changing circumstances; members' roles are varied to accomplish the task as well as maintain a sense of group identity; and communication between members is marked by trust and openness, creating a supportive, rather than defensive, climate. This atmosphere makes it possible to view disagreements as being productive for broadening the scope of the group's information. Finally, effective teams evaluate themselves, critically analyzing both their work habits and their relationships.

The rest of this chapter describes productive actions you can take as a team member to improve the chances of your team functioning effectively. The specific steps include helping your

TABLE 3.1. COMPARISON OF EFFECTIVE AND INEFFECTIVE TEAMS.

Effective Teams	Ineffective Teams
Create a climate which fosters high levels of inclusion, affection, acceptance, support and trust. Individuality is valued.	Create a climate that fosters distrust, suspicion, and defensive reactions. Rigid conformity is promoted.
Clarify goals and discuss them to match individual with group goals. Goals are cooperatively structured.	Accept imposed goals that are competitively structured.
Accept conflict as a sign of members' involvement and quality decision making.	Ignore, deny, avoid, or suppress conflict.
Focus on accomplishing the task and maintaining unity. Participation and leadership are distributed among all group members.	Focus only on task accomplishments. Members' roles are rigid and static. High-authority members dominate.
Match decision-making procedures to the situation. Different methods are used at different times.	Make decisions based on authority. Members' involvement is minimal.
Evaluate the effectiveness of the team and decide how to improve its functioning.	Authority figures evaluate the team's effectiveness. Internal maintenance is ignored as much as possible.

Note: From D.W. Johnson & F.P. Johnson, *Joining Together: Group Theory and Group Skill* (5th ed.) (pp. 64-65). Copyright © 1994 Allyn & Bacon. Adapted by permission.

team to understand the climate created by members' behaviors, clarify group goals and identify hidden agendas, balance accomplishing the task with maintaining group cohesion, and manage problem participants.

UNDERSTANDING THE CLIMATE SURROUNDING BEHAVIOR

Just as different geographical locales can be characterized by their harsh winters or humid summers, different work units within the same organization can be differentiated by their atmospheric conditions. In Production, things might be bright and sunny as they are in Florida today. However, in Sales—as in Kansas—things are a bit stormy. People are arguing and the air is filled with tension. In Accounting, things are a bit cloudy and no one is sure what is going to happen. We use weather analogies to quickly typify the quality of interaction within a work group.

The better your ability to recognize the different signs of the weather, the better your ability to protect yourself from the elements. Understanding how the group climate influences conflict interaction is a necessary component of surviving conflict at work. Your responses to conflict will be influenced not only by individual personalities, but by the "personality" of your work group or project team. It is thus necessary to consider the context surrounding individual behavior.

A work unit's climate, Folger and Poole (1984) explained, is "the relatively enduring quality of the group situation that . . . is experienced in common by group members" (p. 84). In other words, the term *climate* describes the atmosphere created by patterns in how people in a group talk and interact with each other. Climates are created and maintained by particular events in the group interaction (Folger & Poole, 1984). A work unit's climate is relatively enduring, but it can evolve over time.

Although the basic climate within a work unit is not the product of any one individual, the actions of an individual can trigger changes in the group atmosphere if other members follow along. Their actions can build on each other, creating a ripple effect that spreads through the work unit. In the following case study, notice how the climate in the 12-person work unit is subtly altered by the behaviors of the subgroup of Missy, Mike, and Steven.

Case Study 3.1: The Department of Eden

A recent retirement left Linda Marshall's software programming department with a vacancy on short notice. Because the organization was restructuring and cutting vacant positions, Linda Marshall pushed aggressively for a one-year temporary appointment at a lower salary base than the retiring senior-level program-

mer had earned. After one year, the position would be re-evaluated and, presumably, restored to a permanent position.

Melissa Jenkins, fresh out of graduate school, was looking forward to filling this position. She had been competitively selected from a large pool of applicants, but it did not hurt that she graduated from the same school as did the manager of the department. If her performance appraisals during the year were good, Melissa expected a permanent position.

In her first few weeks, her coworkers dropped by her office to introduce themselves and express their delight in having her "on board." Some of them mentioned how they were impressed by her credentials, and others commented enthusiastically about her state-of-the-art computer equipment. To Melissa, the group seemed amicable. The department had a reputation for quality work and each person was encouraged to set their own pace, build on their own style, and thrive in their given area of expertise.

However, it wasn't long before Melissa realized that the freedom of working independently also meant isolation. When she had questions about coordinating her projects with the engineering department or had problems with payroll over her deductions, she realized that her coworkers were entrenched in their own projects and had little interest in advising her about the informal networks within the company. Without friends or family in the area, Melissa's only social contacts were through her job. She discovered that most of her colleagues were somewhat older, had families, and were not very interested in going for a beer after work. Melissa missed the working relationships she'd taken for granted in graduate school—until she got to know the guys at the end of the hall, Mike and Steven.

Mike Alexander was only a few years older than Melissa, but he had been with the company for 5 years. He had a pleasant, engaging manner that sparked camaraderie. His sprightly sense of humor had become more adventuresome since he'd realized his prospects for promotion were slim after refusing a promotion that would have required relocating his family. Steven Landers, Mike's office mate, had been with the company for 15 years, but his position was tenuous. A project team was working with an outside contractor to develop an operating system that would make Steven's area of expertise obsolete. Melissa started to take her breaks in their office. As a long time member of the department, Steven "took her under his wing." Mike and Steven were the only ones in the department who called her "Missy."

Mike, Steven, and Missy began spending time together outside of the office as well. They compared impressions of work, colleagues, and responded to each other's "take" on how the company would change in the face of financial stress. The three quickly became friends and began thinking of practical jokes to lighten up the serious tone of the department meetings.

When a senior programmer was listed in the local newspaper's summary of police activities, the three saw an opportunity. Their colleague was notorious for parking violations and she had paid a $25 fine, which the newspaper dutifully reported. Through skillful cutting, pasting, and xeroxing, Mike, Steven, and Missy transformed the parking violation into a bar room brawl in which an officer was slapped and his shirt was torn. They made photo copies of their creation and distributed them at the next staff meeting.

Their target took the joke in stride, reminding the conspirators that they had better behave or she would slap their faces and tear their clothes. Most of the department enjoyed the light humor and showed that they could take being poked fun at. Linda Marshall didn't discourage the practical jokers because their antics didn't seem to hamper productivity.

No one was immune from the practical jokers—not even the jokers themselves. Steven and Mike set Missy up for a joke early on. About a month before Missy's six-month performance appraisal, Steven informed Missy that their manager, Linda, had come to Steven for some advice on a problematic issue (Steven having the benefit of his greater years of service to the department). It seems that Linda had noticed that Missy had taken to wearing more casual clothes in face of inclement weather. As the "joke" goes, Linda asked Steve how she should deal with Missy.

Missy took it, hook line and sinker. She was shocked and worried about her upcoming performance appraisal. Steven advised her not to do anything—it would just blow over. The point of the joke was to see how long Missy could be strung along and finally surprised with having had one "pulled over" on her.

No one knew when Steven and Mike were planning to spring the joke on Missy, but Linda found out about it when she overheard Mike and Steve talking in the hallway. Linda promptly went to Melissa to clear up the situation. The damage, however, had already been done. Several weeks had gone by with Melissa resenting her supervisor. Furthermore, Melissa was embarrassed at being laughed at behind her back. Although she didn't speak to them directly, Linda was upset with Steven and Mike for creating additional problems for her to solve. Distrust and suspicion had gained a foothold.

*The threesome's later attempts at humor during depart-
ment meetings evolved into thinly veiled barbs at the actions, attitudes, or decisions of others in the department. The targets
responded by sniping back at the jokers or remaining silent on
issues about which they had usually been outspoken. As individuals made their progress reports, others would carry on side conversations, read the newspaper, or doodle on their note pads. The
serious tone of department meetings had become tense. Minor matters such as the Christmas party and the company bowling league
took forever to dispense with, and substantive issue were frequently tabled until the next meeting.*

*The mood of the company on the whole was growing
strained. Attempts at getting clear, timely decisions from upper
management resulted in false leads and flared tempers. As an
active member in the department, it was difficult for Melissa not to
know about the fluctuations in management priorities and internal
wrangling. What had once seemed to be a "sure thing" had turned
into a series of misplaced hopes and exercises in futility. Melissa—
frustrated and disillusioned—decided to accept a position else-
where. Once again, Linda Marshall found herself arguing for a
temporary replacement.*

As you can see in the "Department of Eden," the atmosphere within a work unit is created by subtle factors. We can,
however, identify four themes around which the details revolve:
the nature of power relationships, the type of relationships or
interdependence between team members, the sense of group
identity, and the degree of supportiveness (Folger & Poole, 1984).

The *distribution of power* among team members shapes
the nature of the work-unit climate. Mike and Steven's marginal
positions within the department and the broader organization set
the stage for their "adoption" of Missy and their indirect efforts at
control. By coopting the "new kid," Mike and Steven strengthened
their coalition and gained the attention, appreciation, and connections of a well-credentialed, albeit naive, colleague in Missy.
Their use of the diminutive form of her name illustrated the hierarchy within the subgroup.

Missy's inexperience within the organization and the workplace made her particularly vulnerable to their manipulations.
The common bond they shared was their relative powerlessness.
Lacking tangible avenues of influence, the threesome resorted to
indirect methods of control, using humor to cover their challenges
to the established power relationships in the work unit.

To understand the distribution of power within your work team, you should ask the following questions: Is power shared or concentrated in the hands of a few people? Does power shift according to the task and members' information and expertise, or is the power structure rigidly static? Are the same types of decision-making procedures used all the time or are they adapted to suit different circumstances? How do individuals attempt to gain power or control over others in the group? (Folger & Poole, 1984).

You should also consider the *type of interdependence* between group members. A cooperative orientation develops when members perceive that they can accomplish their individual objectives only by working together. Group goals and individual goals mesh. In contrast, a competitive orientation develops when individuals perceive that they can only accomplish their objectives if others are prevented from accomplishing their goals. A third orientation, individualistic, exists when group members perceive that their objectives are unrelated to the actions of others (Johnson & Johnson, 1991).

It is important to consider whether the type of working relationships within a team are appropriate given the experience level of the participants and the nature of the task. Linda Marshall's programming group, for example, initially displayed an individualistic orientation that was appropriate for those who had been with the company for years. Melissa, however, as a new hire, needed the connections that a cooperative environment could provide. She found such a cooperative environment, or so it appeared, in the subgroup of Mike and Steven, until their joke on Melissa illustrated the competitive undercurrents in the relationships among the three.

To analyze the type of interdependence in your work team, you might ask yourself the following questions: Do members work as individuals or as part of a team? Does one person's gain come at the expense of another? Are members rewarded for competition or cooperation? A survey at the end of this chapter provides more detail about each of these three orientations and might help you identify your own preferences as well as the dominant orientation of your work unit or project team.

Another factor determining the nature of the group climate is the *sense of group identity,* or the degree to which members feel committed to the group. Do members share responsibility for decisions? Do members feel ownership of the group's accomplishments? An individualistic orientation such as that in the "Department of Eden" usually means that the members' sense of group identity is relatively weak; individuals focus on their own goals more than on working as a group. A weak sense of group identity makes it easier for individual actions to over-shadow the more enduring qualities of the group. In our case study, the actions of a subgroup were enough to shift members' perceptions of the prevailing climate from "live and let live" to "let's get the other guy."

Finally, it is important to assess the *degree of supportive-ness* within a team. You should consider the following questions: Are members friendly with each other? Can members trust one another? Can members safely express emotions in the group? Does the group tolerate disagreements? To what degree does the group emphasize task and relationship concerns? (Folger & Poole, 1984). Effective teams develop a climate in which open, honest communication is the norm, not the exception.

Mike and Steven's "joke" on Melissa was threatening in a way that the trio's joke on the senior programmer was not. All were invited to laugh along in the first practical joke; it was above-board. The second joke, on the other hand, played on fears that others will whisper behind our backs. It destroyed a basic precondition for trust—the assumption that people will speak directly to those with whom they have problems. The second joke was critical in undermining the level of supportiveness within the subgroup. For Missy, the joke also brought questions she had about her supervisor Linda Marshall to the surface.

The climate within "The Department of Eden" led mem-bers to expect certain actions and responses toward disagree-ments. These expectations evolved into realities as members acted on the basis of imagined outcomes. Thus, the climate in a work unit is important because it serves to intensify interaction. Cooperative climates invite cooperative behaviors, Deutsch (1969) found, whereas competitive climates invite competitive behaviors. The climate in a work unit becomes a gauge against which we measure our own behaviors.

When power is rigidly centralized, the degree of supportive-ness is low, and the sense of group identity weak, we expect con-flict interactions to escalate. Control and conformity become domi-nant concerns, prompting hidden agendas and indirect methods of influence. In such an environment, avoiding overt conflict is more likely. As we mentioned in chapter 2, however, you will need to decide when the issue is worth the effort and potential damage to relationships before initiating direct confrontations.

On the other hand, when power is equalized among team members, the sense of group identity is high, and the members of the group are supportive of one another, conflict episodes tend to focus more on substantive issues and less on establishing an individual's status within the group. In such instances, a problem-solving orientation is more likely to emerge. Constructive conflict interaction is more likely in such environments.

Although a basic, generally established organizational or departmental climate may be beyond any individual's control, you can have a significant impact on your immediate environment. Remember that "small, cumulative changes in interaction can eventually result in major changes in climate" (Folger & Poole, 1984, p. 175). Think about how you communicate with group members and practice supportive communication as we explained it in chapter 2. Use inclusive pronouns such as "we" and "our," rather than "me" and "mine." One person's constructive actions can have a ripple effect on the group's climate, just as the destructive actions in the case study had a negative effect.

Second, in attempting to influence the climate in your work unit, you can chose to openly discuss the themes that trouble you. As Folger and Poole (1984) explained, "Much of a climate's influence on group interaction depends on members' inability to recognize it" (p. 176). If you can talk about the impact of the climate, group members can make conscious choices to adapt their interaction patterns. Sometimes an individual can trigger alterations in group interaction by initiating a discussion of unrecognized habits.

Finally, if you are a gambler, you might decide on a riskier tactic for changing a group's climate by trying to create a critical incident that shifts the group's attention and forces alterations in interaction patterns. Linda Marshall, for example, might have chosen to wear torn jeans and a stained t-shirt to a department meeting to initiate a group discussion of expectations about appropriate dress. Clearly, the issue must be important, and the timing is crucial. Even so, creating a critical incident is a risky tactic and should be reserved as a last resort.

We believe that developing a climate that fosters productive responses to conflict can be achieved if team members consciously monitor their own actions as well as the unspoken assumptions that guide group behavior. In the next section, we examine one of the most common unspoken assumptions team members make—agreement on goals. In addition to understanding the context surrounding behavior, you should help your team to clarify goals and deal with hidden agendas.

CLARIFYING GOALS AND IDENTIFYING HIDDEN AGENDAS

On the surface, the goals of a project team or work unit might seem so obvious that no discussion is required. Many of us unquestioningly accept that "We're all here to get a job done." We assume that the stated reasons for calling a group into being are clear and unambiguous. Reality, however, is seldom so clear-cut. All too often, work teams assume agreement on goals when there actually is none.

Any work team or unit represents a blending of individual objectives and organizational goals. However, individual and group goals do not always overlap; in fact, the two can be in direct conflict. At any point in group interaction, there are likely to be individual agendas operating beneath the surface agenda. These hidden agendas, or private and unspoken concerns, are still very much a part of the group's concern.

Hidden agendas frequently result in nonoperational goals that are broad and vague. By moving discussion toward generalities such as "full employment" or "universal health coverage," members can stay in their safety zones. There can be a lot of words, but few actions other than vague resolutions. Operational goals, in contrast, are specific and targeted toward well-defined outcomes. The specific steps to achieve the goal are clear. For this reason, operational goals help focus the group's activities and make it relatively easy to define that which has been accomplished. Agreement on clear operational goals is a key component of effectiveness.

In addition, hidden agendas can affect how the group deals with its stated agenda. Groups may find that their work on the stated agenda is stalled by constant digressions or plagued by a lack of following through, as was the case in "The Department of Eden." The group avoided dealing with residual feelings about the practical jokes.

Recognizing that hidden agendas might be operating is a necessary first step in dealing with them. To identify signs that hidden agendas are operating beneath the surface within your work group, look for the following signs of avoidance:

- People "tune out" of the interaction.
- The group loses interest in solving the problem.
- Suggested solutions are quickly accepted.
- Members stop themselves from raising controversial aspects of an issue.

- Unresolved issues keep emerging in the same or different form.
- Discussion centers on a safe aspect of a broader and more explosive issue.
- Little sharing of information occurs.
- Outspoken members are notably quiet.
- No plans are made to implement a chosen solution. (Folger & Poole, 1984, p. 78)

Instead of becoming impatient with hidden agendas, you should accept them as a fact of organizational life. It is natural that members of a group will see things differently and have different priorities. In many instances, it is helpful to bring hidden agendas to the surface through procedures that invite individuals to air their concerns. For example, suggesting that everyone comment on how they feel about a proposal before a vote might serve to clear the air and identify unrecognized issues. Soliciting consistent feedback about members' perceptions of the group's progress is also helpful. Sometimes anonymous, written evaluations help to bring hidden agendas to the surface.

Finally, it is important to recognize that not all hidden agendas can be discussed openly. As we mentioned in chapter 2, there a number of factors to consider in deciding whether to confront conflict. The importance of the issue must be weighed against an assessment of the strength of relationships. Considering the climate of interaction is also important—if the climate is competitive, a discussion of hidden agendas might simply lead to escalation. In a individualistic environment, individuals may use such a discussion to dissolve the group.

Knowing when to confront hidden agendas is an important judgment call because "clearing the air," although often necessary, can personalize conflicts as the differences between issues and individuals get blurred. Evaluative statements can prompt defensive responses, creating a negative communication climate. The stress of acknowledging opposing stands can cause people to "freeze," to cling inflexibly to their initial public stances on an issue.

For these reasons, it is important to recognize the signs of destructive conflict spirals:

- An issue takes much longer to deal with than was anticipated.
- Members repeatedly offer the same arguments.
- Mounting tension is felt in the group.

- The group gets nowhere but seems to be working feverishly.
- Name calling and personal arguments are used.
- Threats are used to win arguments.
- Coalitions emerge as members become polarized on the issue.
- Less direct eye contact occurs between members.
- Sarcastic humor is used as a form of tension release.
- Heated disagreements about trivial issues dominate the discussion.
- Ideas are attacked before they are completely expressed.
- Members accuse one another of not understanding the basic issue.
- Members distort one another's contributions. (Folger & Poole, 1984, p. 78)

When you see these signs of escalation, you might suggest a break in the group's interaction, or suggest an alternative method or procedure.

Successful conflict management requires that people clarify their differences while maintaining their ability to appreciate their similarities, recognize their common goals, and create action to manage their conflict. Groups in conflict tend to vacillate between avoidance and escalation, each of which carries it own problems. The following behaviors are positive signs that disputants are working through conflict and moving in productive directions:

- Feelings and emotions are acknowledged rather than denied.
- Differences are discussed openly as the group explores the causes behind conflict.
- Dissent can be freely expressed; opposing opinions are sought as a part of the clarification process.
- Decision making is marked by the sharing of information.
- Feedback is solicited and mechanisms for appraising ongoing work habits are developed.
- Members are flexible in their behaviors, particularly when it comes to means for managing differences.
- Members express commitment to all parties accomplishing their goals.
- Participation level is high.

In sum, productive conflict interaction is more likely if the group develops a supportive climate, clarifies goals, and recognizes hidden agendas. You need to understand not only your own goals, but how other group members view their individual goals in relation to the group goals and need to consider what you want to get out of and give to this group. In addition, you should encourage discussion of the question, "How will we work together to get the task done?" Effective teams spend time discussing their goals, even when goals are prescribed by upper management. It is important for members to clarify their different individual perceptions about goals and "reword, reorganize, and review the goals until the majority of members feel a sense of 'ownership' toward them" (Johnson & Johnson, 1991, p. 71).

BALANCING ACCOMPLISHING THE TASK WITH MAINTAINING UNITY

Effective teams are marked by shared leadership and power. They balance a concern with accomplishing the task with an interest in creating and maintaining a sense of group identity. Ineffective teams, in contrast, rely on centralized power and focus only on the task. Ironically, this task focus creates an atmosphere in which members do not feel safe discussing ideas. A single-minded focus on the task inhibits the very goal it is supposed to achieve.

In this section, we describe the specific behaviors that have to occur to manage a group thought line and maintain commitment to the work unit. We also highlight common problems in decision making to watch for during times of overt conflict.

Accomplishing the Task

Problem solving or decision making is a continuing pattern of relationships among members of the work unit; a pattern over which every individual member has significant influence. It is amazing the effect a bit of information here, a loud objection there, a question of clarification, or a request for information can have on an impending decision. Table 3.2 indicates several roles that individuals can adopt that are directed at initiating and expediting tasks. In addition, the table indicates roles that are usually destructive.

TABLE 3.2. TASK ROLES.

Usually Helpful	Usually Destructive
Initiating: Proposes tasks or goals; defines a group problem; suggests a procedure or ideas for solving a problem.	Waits for others to initiate; withholds ideas or suggestions.
Seeking information: Requests facts; seeks relevant information about a group problem or concern; is aware of need for information.	Is unaware of need for facts, or of what is relevant to the problem or task at hand.
Giving information: Offers facts; provides relevant information about a group concern.	Avoids facts; prefers to state personal opinions or prejudices.
Seeking opinions: Asks for expression of feeling; requests statements of estimate, expressions of value; seeks suggestions and ideas.	Does not ask what others wish or think; considers other opinions irrelevant.
Giving opinions: States belief about a matter before the group; gives ideas and suggestions.	States own opinion whether relevant or not; withholds opinions or ideas when needed by the group.
Clarifying: Interprets ideas or suggestions; clears up confusion; defines needed terms; indicates alternatives and issues confronting the group.	Is unaware or irritated by confusion or ambiguities; ignores the confusion of others.
Elaborating: Gives examples, develops meanings; makes generalizations; indicates how a proposal might work out if adopted.	Is inconsiderate of those who do not understand; refuses to explain, show new meaning.
Summarizing: Pulls together related ideas; restates suggestions after the group has discussed them; offers decision or conclusions for the group to accept or reject.	Moves ahead without checking for relationship or integration of ideas; lets people make their own integrations or relationships.
Testing Consensus: Asks if the group is nearing a decision; checks with members to assess how much agreement has been reached.	Assumes silence equals agreement. Attends to own needs; Does not note group direction; complains about slow progress.

From *Groups: Theory and Experience* (3rd ed.) (pp. 282-283) by R.W. Napier and M.K. Gershenfeld. Copyright © 1985 by Houghton Mifflin. Reprinted by permission.

Does the list of usually destructive behaviors sound familiar? Decision making is a difficult process of coordinating and clarifying ideas. Some groups become paralyzed when confronted with a decision because no one initiates ideas; some argue interminably over a minor point because no one is clarifying or summarizing; others rush into a vote, only to reverse their decision later because no one tested for consensus.

These problems result when members rely too much on information giving and opinion giving without paying attention to coordinating and blending ideas. The necessary task roles that are too often overlooked include clarifying, elaborating, summarizing, and testing consensus. When you see a work group having trouble making decisions, you should focus on those functions that coordinate ideas, not on the information and opinions.

Avoiding Trained Incapacities

In addition, you should be aware of the common mistakes that plague groups during times of conflict. Too often, we rely on ritualistic ways of getting the job done. During conflict interaction, relying on what has worked in the past can actually worsen the situation. Our past training in decision making causes us to misjudge the present situation. During conflict episodes, our normal work habits can easily become more harmful than helpful. Managing conflict between coworkers requires the ability to recognize when normally useful work habits have to be abandoned because they encourage destructive conflict cycles.

The *typical procedures* that work units employ can make confrontation inevitable or suppress creative ideas. For example, parliamentary procedure, with its implicit expectation of a vote, can lead to polarization. The "either or" structure in the procedure forecloses better alternatives from consideration. When this formal procedure is employed during conflict interaction, it has the impact of foreclosing minority opinion, creating fertile grounds for escalation cycles.

Our typical procedures can also function to suppress creative ideas as group members tend to jump toward solutions before adequate analysis. Evaluative judgments so necessary in the final stages of decision making can inhibit creative ideas from emerging. It helps if you are familiar with a range of different procedures to structure interaction and equalize power. We have included a number of different group procedures you can use to restructure interaction during group meetings at the end of this chapter. You should not be afraid to suggest deviations from typical methods, particularly if you recognize the signs of avoidance or escalation.

Although we have asserted that clear operational goals are a hallmark of successful teams, there is a time when *goal centeredness* can be counterproductive. Focusing only on the task can become a real problem when it prevents the group from developing as a cohesive unit. During conflict interaction, a task focus can make you overlook legitimate individual needs. Similarly, neglecting the relationships between group members can allow frustrations to fester until they explode in dramatic ways or emerge indirectly through scapegoating. If goal centeredness is used to hurry the group along and suppress differences, this normally functional work habit can fan the flames of conflict interaction.

Selecting appropriate procedures for decision making is an important step in avoiding its common pitfalls. In addition, the group as a whole must have a variety of task functions represented. You can help your work unit or project team function effectively by recognizing which functions or roles are overrepresented and which are underrepresented. In this way, you will be helping the group to work smarter rather than harder.

Fostering Commitment to the Work Unit

In addition to accomplishing their task, an effective work group must develop *a sense of group identity*. Members must feel commitment to the group and share a sense of responsibility for its decisions. Maintaining a commitment to the group is an important part of "getting the job done." There are several actions that individuals can take to promote positive interactions and encourage participation (see Table 3.3).

The specific behaviors that help foster a sense of group unity involve smoothing out minor differences between members, encouraging a supportive atmosphere, relieving tension, and promoting individuals' sense of being part of the unit. All too often in work teams, following and relieving tension through sarcastic humor are overrepresented. What gets ignored are the roles of gate keeping, standard setting, and calling attention to the feelings present in the group.

Maintaining work group unity has a great deal to do with practicing supportive, rather than defensive, communication. It also involves recognizing that discussions shouldn't always be so serious that people cannot enjoy themselves. Enjoying the group is a part of functioning effectively.

TABLE 3.3. GROUP BUILDING AND MAINTENANCE ROLES.

Usually Helpful	Usually Destructive
Encouraging: Is friendly, warm and responsive to others; accepts others and their contributions.	Is cold, unresponsive, unfriendly; rejects others' contribution; ignores them.
Expressing Feelings: Expresses feelings present in the group; calls attention of the group to its reaction to ideas and suggestions; expresses own feelings.	Ignores the reaction of the group as whole; refuses to express own feeling when needed or asked.
Harmonizing: Attempts to reconcile disagreements; reduces tension through humorous, relaxing comments; gets people to explore their differences and find common ground.	Irritates or "needles" others; encourages disagreement for its own sake; uses emotion-laden words.
Compromising: When own idea or status is involved in a conflict, offers compromise, yields status, admits error; disciplines self to maintain group cohesion.	Becomes defensive, haughty; withdraws or walks out; demands subservience or submission from others.
Gate Keeping: Attempts to keep communication channels open, facilitates the participation of others, and suggests procedures that permit discussing group problems.	Ignores miscommunications; fails to listen to others; ignores the group needs that are expressed.
Setting Standards or Goals: Expresses standards or goals for group to achieve; helps the group become aware of unspoken assumptions.	Goes own way; is irrelevant; ignores group standards or goals and direction.
Following: Goes along with movement of the group; accepts ideas of others; listens to and serves as an interested audience.	Participates on own ideas but does not actively listen to others; looks for loopholes in ideas; is carping.

From *Groups: Theory and Experience* (3rd ed.) (pp. 283-284) by R.W. Napier and M.K. Gershenfeld. Copyright © 1985 by Houghton Mifflin Co. Reprinted by permission.

MANAGING CONFLICT AS IT ERUPTS IN MEETINGS

Despite everyone's best efforts, problem behaviors will still emerge during the process of working together. We conclude this chapter by considering how you might respond to problem participants in ways that increase your chances of turning destructive behavior in more constructive directions. We suggest that you keep in mind the following principles:

Don't mirror behavior. Be careful not to fall into the trap of letting the problem person dictate the group's activities. Try not to respond in kind to the behavior of the problem participant; instead, attempt to side step the problem behavior, turning the interaction in an unexpected direction. By giving an unexpected response, you will deny the "payoff" for problem behavior.

Be sensitive to the group climate. Recognize that problem behavior might be the tip of a potential iceberg. The person who is creating a problem reflects, to a certain degree, the underlying group dynamics. A problem participant can provide important clues to unrecognized problems. For this reason, it is often effective to "level" with a problem participant because confronting rather than ignoring troubling behavior helps establish a norm of open, honest communication. Your first priority should be the impact your actions will have on the overall group climate.

Use group-centered power resources rather than individual-centered power resources. Effective teams equalize power and share leadership tasks. Although we discuss power dynamics in more detail in the next chapter, you should recognize that power resources such as knowledge and information, which are accessible by all group members, are likely to be more effective than rewards or punishment, which are available to only a few. Power moves based on formal authority or imposing your position through "one-upping" to win an immediate ego battle are not productive if you irreparably harm the ongoing relationships among team members and create a defensive climate. The group's interest in accomplishing a common goal is the greatest resource you have in dealing with problem participants, and developing a common goal has a lot to do with encouraging group-centered power resources.

Consider future implications of your actions. Problem individuals usually do not disappear; you are likely to have to deal with this individual in the future. It is thus always wise to allow room for "saving face." Difficult behavior is frequently prompted by concerns about our "image" in the minds of coworkers, subordinates, and superiors. Sometimes, problem participants can be managed by substituting positive strokes for the negative strokes that a problem individual encourages through their behaviors. Providing a way for a person to maintain their sense of respect is an important part of avoiding a cycle of recrimination designed to regain status in the group.

Although it is impossible to anticipate every bizarre behavior that can occur in a work team, we have provided some profiles of common behaviors that are irritating, can undermine the group's sense of unity, and can sabotage efforts at decision making. In the following discussion, we suggest how you might apply these principles to deal with difficult individuals in ways that increase the chances of productive interaction.

The Show-Off knows a great deal about the topic, desires to exhibit in-depth knowledge, and dominates the discussion in doing so. There is nothing anyone can tell this person that they haven't already heard or read about. Although it is extremely tempting to try to knock the show-off down a peg or two, this effort is likely to backfire by creating a competitive, defensive atmosphere, particularly in the minds of other less articulate or experienced group members.

To deal with a show-off, you should swallow your pride and recognize the show-off's need for positive strokes. Suggest that their knowledge could enable them to take the lead on an important project. If the show-off continues to dominate discussion, you should attempt to pull other group members into the conversation. Avoid looking directly at the show-off because eye contact tends to encourage people to continue talking. Wait until the show-off pauses, offer a quick compliment, then ask another member to respond ("You've been clear about what worked for you, Jim; did you have a similar experience in your work, Don?").

The Eager Beaver is like a puppy dog eager to please, attempting to comment on every point, but in doing so, keeping other members from participating. Unlike the show-off's, their motive is simply to help the group, so you don't want to shoot the Eager Beaver down. Instead, you might manage such members by tactfully interrupting them and asking direct questions of other members "Dave, I really appreciate your ideas. Now let's see what someone else might contribute; Karen, what do you think would apply to this?" (Andrews & Baird, 1990, p. 311). When the Eager Beaver volunteers for more assignments than they can possibly handle, point out the need to equalize the work load.

The Heckler argues about every point being made, pointing out the limitations of each proposal, and limits the group's ability to brainstorm ideas because of the consistently critical comments that are leveled at the group. Left unchecked, the Heckler hampers the group's ability to accomplish anything, because there's always something wrong with any suggestions.

In dealing with the Heckler, it's important to remain calm and not heckle back. Agree with legitimate objections the Heckler raises, but toss extreme points to the group for discussion (e.g., "Does anyone else have problem with this proposal?"). Usually, the group will quickly reject the objections of the Heckler. If it continues, you may ask the Heckler to suggest positive points. "I've heard a number of things you do not support; what actions would you view positively?" The silence that usually follows illustrates the Heckler's inability to generate positive, rather than negative, ideas.

The Whisperers carry on side conversations that may be related to the subject at hand, but are distracting to the group as a whole. Don't embarrass Whisperers by reacting like a first-grade teacher. Instead, assume the Whisperer has an important point for the group to hear; ask them to share it. "I'm sorry . . . I didn't hear you. Could you repeat that?" If the behavior is consistent, sit between Whisperers or change the physical arrangements.

The Exploder precipitates a shouting tirade. The volume quickly becomes unbearable, and the less assertive members of the group become intimidated into silence. Be careful not to respond by escalating the intensity of your comments. Instead, in a quiet, controlled manner, you should address the tone of the Exploder's comments. Begin by acknowledging the legitimacy of the Exploder's emotions: "I understand you are upset about this." Then, point out the counterproductive nonverbals that interfere with the message (i.e., a pounding fist, rapid-fire rate of speech, and a loud tone): "Although I understand that you are legitimately upset about this, it is very difficult for me to focus on your point when you are shouting. Please, slow down and lower your voice."

The Mule refuses to move beyond one point. After attempting to explain a different point of view to the obstinate participant, you might ask other members if they have similar concerns. If so, the issue must be resolved before going any further. If not, remind the obstinate participant of the group's agenda and point out that time is limited. Suggest alternative avenues for the obstinate participant to pursue if the issue is really important to them. "Since you have real problems with Accounting's method of valuing your inventory, why don't you talk to the Vice-President. Here, I'll get the number for you."

The Sniper uses sarcasm or humor to take public pot shots at coworkers or the group leader. Unlike the Heckler, who argues about every point being made, the Sniper focuses on other individuals. For example, when a group member arrives 10 minutes late to a meeting, the Sniper might start in with "Nice of you to join us." If the target attempts a defense, the sniper responds with "Can't you take a joke?"

The Sniper will always win a snideness dual, so don't attempt to mirror the behavior. In responding to the Sniper, separate the tone from the explicit content of the "snipe." "You have a legitimate gripe about lateness. I'm sorry I was delayed, but I'm concerned about the edge to your comment. Are you upset about a more basic issue?" Such an approach illustrates your willingness to listen to criticism while reinforcing a norm of dealing directly rather than indirectly with relationship issues.

The Rambler talks about everything under the sun except the subject at hand, leading discussions into endless digressions and presenting an obstacle to the group's progress. Recognize the Rambler's behavior as an unconscious bid for attention. Don't embarrass the individual by displaying excessive impatience—wait for the Rambler to pause to breathe, thank him or her for the comments, restate a relevant point to the discussion, and go on.

The Professional Griper monopolizes the discussion by listing everything that he or she feels is wrong with the place. Frequently, complainers gripe about other people behind their backs or whine about policies beyond your control. Politely point out the limits of your authority. "It would be nice, Bob, if we ruled the world, but we don't. Our problem is to focus on X." If the Griper persists in complaining about individuals behind their backs, look them in the eye and say, "I don't agree, but I'm concerned about the intensity of your feelings. I'd be happy to help you mediate this problem by reflecting your feelings to Y. Now, let's get to the point at hand."

The Off-Base Participant is heading in a direction that is clearly wrong. Such individuals can unintentionally spread confusion throughout the group. Don't embarrass them because we all make mistakes. Instead, take the blame on yourself. Say, "Something I said must have led you off the subject. This is the direction in which we were heading" or, "That's one way of looking at it, but how can we reconcile that with . . . " (stating the correct point).

SUMMARY

The trend toward corporate restructuring and employee "empow-erment" places a premium on your ability to manage conflict between you and your coworkers. It is increasingly important for you to recognize the characteristics of effective work teams and be able to enact a wide variety of roles. Effective teams result when members jointly take responsibility for managing the group process. In this chapter, we explained the factors that shape group interaction and suggested actions you can take to facilitate effective problem solving and coordination among team members.

First, you need to analyze the climate surrounding group interaction. The atmosphere within the team creates expectations that provide standards for gauging behaviors. We suggested that you consider the nature of the power relationships in the group, the type of interdependence among group members, the level of commitment to the group, and the degree of supportiveness. By assessing these factors, you can place behaviors in context, choosing to alter your actions or initiate discussion of trouble spots.

A second step you can take is to *not* assume that group goals are clear to all members and commonly agreed on. Hidden agendas are a fact of life, and the group needs to manage them in some fashion. We identified specific behaviors that can help you decide when a group is avoiding, escalating, or working productively on individual agendas. Deciding how and when to confront hidden agendas is a judgment call, but clarifying operational goals on which team members agree is an important step in creating effective teams.

A third element to consider is the balance between task and group maintenance concerns. Any team must both accomplish a task and maintain a sense of group identity. To help you diagnose the behaviors in your work teams, we delineated the specific components of effective decision making and group cohesion. When it comes to the task, team members all too often rely on information and opinions, neglecting to coordinate and blend ideas through clarifying, elaborating, and testing consensus. In terms of group-building functions, team members often rely too much on following and tension relieving—ignoring gate keeping, standard setting, and talking about feelings. You can help a team function more effectively by performing the roles that are under-represented in the group process.

Finally, we considered ways in which you can attempt to manage problem behaviors in meetings. We suggested that you avoid mirroring behavior; responding to a snipe with a snipe, for example. You should consider the consequences of your actions on the group climate as a whole, rather than letting the problem person become your sole focus. Whenever you deal with problem participants, you should consider the future implications of your actions, allowing room for individuals to save face, and thus avoid cycles of recrimination. We also suggested that you use group-centered power resources such as knowledge and information, rather than relying on formal authority. Because of the important role that power plays in conflict interaction, we focus on this issue in the next chapter.

DISCUSSION QUESTIONS

1. How would you describe the climate in your organization? Does it facilitate or inhibit successful decision making?
2. What additional characteristics of effective work teams would you add to the list?
3. What do performance appraisals in your organization reward—cooperation, competition, or individualism?
4. Do you consider yourself effective in dealing with difficult employees? Why or why not?
5. What additional profiles of problem participants can you add? How would or did you handle them?
6. What types of hidden agendas have you seen operating in your workplace? Would confronting them be appropriate? How would you initiate such a discussion?
7. What additional methods or procedures have you found to be effective for accomplishing different types of work group tasks?

EXERCISES

Assessing Your Orientation Toward Teamwork (From D.W. Johnson & F.P. Johnson, *Joining Together: Group Theory and Group Skills (s/e)*. Copyright © 1994 by Allyn & Bacon. Reprinted with permission.)

For each item below, indicate your general perceptions about each statement. In the appropriate space, write down the number that most accurately describes your actions. 1 = *Never*, 2 = *Seldom*, 3 = *Sometimes*, 4 = *Mostly*, 5 = *Always*. Using the scoring table that follows the questionnaire, determine your score.

1. ____ I like to compare myself with others to see who is best.
2. ____ In my situation, people spend a lot of time working by themselves.
3. ____ In my situation, people share their ideas and resources with each other.
4. ____ In my situation, people are motivated to see who can do the best job.
5. ____ In my situation, individuals like to work by themselves.
6. ____ In my situation, individuals learn lots of important things from each other.
7. ____ In my situation, individuals want to do better than others.
8. ____ In my situation, it bothers individuals when they have to work with each other.
9. ____ In my situation, individuals help each other do a good job.
10. ____ In my situation, individuals are encouraged to outperform each other.
11. ____ In my situation, individuals would rather work alone than work together.
12. ____ In my situation, individuals believe that they are more productive when they work with each other.

Scoring Tables

Competitive	Individualistic	Cooperative
1. ____	2. ____	3. ____
4. ____	5. ____	6. ____
7. ____	8. ____	9. ____
10. ____	11. ____	12. ____
____ Total	____ Total	____ Total

Procedures for Problem Solving

Generating Ideas

1. Brainstorming

When to Use:	If the problem is specific and fairly limited in range.
	If the problem has many answers.
	If the group's immediate purpose is to produce a range of options for later evaluation. The assumption is that quantity breeds quality.

How to Use:	1.	The facilitator explains the problem to be brainstormed.
	2.	The facilitator explains the rules: free associate, postpone judgment, hitchhike on others' suggestions.
	3.	Members suggest as many ideas as possible in the time allotted.
	4.	Someone records all the ideas that are suggested.

2. Nominal Group Technique (silent brainstorming)

When to Use:	If some members tend to dominate.
	If status differences in the group inhibit equal participation. This procedures gives less assertive members an equal voice.

How to Use:	1.	Members silently generate ideas in writing.
	2.	Each individual offers one item in a round-robin listing of items for all to see.
	3.	Ideas are discussed for clarification and understanding.
	4.	Individuals vote in writing on the priority of items.

Building Involvement/Understanding

1. Buzz or Huddle Groups

When to Use: When wide participation is needed in a group that is too large to make vigorous interchange possible or likely.

How to Use: 1. The facilitator presents a clear, limited and specific task to the whole group; sets time limits; and asks for a reporter from each subgroup at the end of the time period.
2. The facilitator suggests how the large group is to be divided or actually makes the division.
3. The leader tells when the allotted time is up, calls the whole group together again and obtains reports from all the groups. The leader lists the suggestions on the board, asking each group to present its list even if it has duplications of items that are already listed.

Implementing Change

1. Program Evaluation and Review Technique (Pert)

When to use: This procedure is effective if the group needs some mathematical estimate of the time required and the probabilities of meeting deadlines. It helps to detect probable bottlenecks, allocate personnel appropriately, estimate reasonable deadlines, and determine necessary starting times.

How to use: 1. Stipulate the final event or occurrence marking the completion of the program.
2. List events that must happen before the final event can happen. What steps or events must occur?

3. Determine necessary, immediate, and preceding events. This step calls for an ordering of events over time.
4. Develop a diagram showing the connection of events.
5. Enumerate activities to place between events.
6. Estimate the times required. Three estimates are made: the most optimistic, the most likely, and the most pessimistic.
7. Compare expected completion times with necessary completion time.
8. Calculate the probabilities of satisfactory completion based on the "critical path" from start to final event.

2. "RISK" Technique

When to use: To test reactions to proposed changes in policy, procedures, or methods before final decisions are made. To reduce misunderstanding, resistance, or problems from such changes when they are imposed from above.

How to use:
1. Present in detail the proposed change to the group.
2. Explain the purpose and procedures of the RISK technique, emphasizing the nonevaluative role of the facilitator.
3. Invite and list all risks, fears, problems, doubts, concerns, etc. The facilitator should allow no evaluation and make none. Allow plenty of time. Often the most significant items do not come until late in the session, often after periods of silence.

4. After the initial meeting, reproduce and circulate the list to all participants, inviting any additions.
5. At the next meeting of the group, add any further risks mentioned.
6. Have the *group* decide if each risk is serious and substantive. No risk should now be considered the property of its presenters, but of the entire group. Often discussants can resolve many of each other's fears, doubts, etc.
7. Remaining risks are now processed into an agenda. The remaining problems can be dealt with one at a time in problem-solving discussions.

REFERENCES

Andrews, P.H., & Baird, J.E. (1992). *Communication for business and the professions* (5th ed.). Dubuque, IA: Wm. C. Brown.

Deutsch, M. (1969). Conflicts: Productive and destructive. *The Journal of Social Issues, 25*(1), 7-41.

Folger, J.P., & Poole, M.S. (1984). *Working through conflict: A communication perspective.* Glenview, IL: Scott, Foresman & Co.

Johnson, D.W., & F.P. Johnson. (1994). *Joining together: Group theory and group skills* (5th ed.). Englewood Cliffs, NJ: Prentice-Hall.

Napier, R.W., & Gershenfeld, M.K. (1985). *Groups: Theory and experience* (3rd ed.). Boston: Houghton Mifflin.

Stern, A. (1993, July 18). Managing by teams is not always as easy as it looks. *New York Times,* p. F5.

▶ 4

Managing Change When You Are "In Charge"

INTRODUCTION

In the previous two chapters, we've discussed strategies for dealing with conflicts between coworkers working on a relatively level playing field. However, many conflicts in the work place occur between those of unequal status. Power differentials warp the playing field, creating undercurrents that shape our behaviors in disputes. How do you cope with conflicts when you are "in charge?" What can you do when subordinates ignore your authority or superiors expect you to enforce inane edicts? Opening up creative options for action requires understanding the power resources available to you and to the "other."

In this chapter, we focus on the power dynamics operating in conflict situations. We begin by defining power and identifying its sources as well as some of the tactics people employ. We then describe how these tactics combine to form strategies or styles of conflict management and provide suggestions about when avoiding might be more appropriate than forcing. We conclude by discussing the pitfalls inherent in positions of strength and of weakness, focusing on how effective managers use power. Our goal is to help you develop a broader repertoire of coping strategies for surviving conflicts at work.

WHAT IS POWER?

While most of us think of power in tangible terms of the ability to reward or punish, power dynamics actually operate in more subtle and diffuse ways. Power is "a kind of force or energy that has the potential to shape the behavior of organizational members" (Frank & Brownell, 1989, p. 406). More simply, power is "the capacity to act" (Jamesway, 1981, p. 87) or "the ability to affect outcomes and goals" (Tjosvold, 1985, p. 282). Although it is tempting to view power as a possession conferred with job titles, this viewpoint is misleading. Having formal authority does not necessarily mean that you are powerful. As a supervisor, for example, you have the right to evaluate employees, but if your negative performance evaluation of an employee is overturned when the employee appeals to your boss, your formal authority is not backed by power.

A necessary first step in dealing with power is recognizing that you participate in its renewal. Without your conscious or unconscious endorsement, no power move will be effective. If a team leader sets a deadline and the employees accept this without question, the power of the designated leader has been endorsed. On the other hand, if one member refuses to go along with the deadline, it might undermine the other members' willingness to go along as well. Power moves must be reinforced by subsequent interactions in order to be effective.

Power springs from relationships among people, the product of subtle and often unspoken negotiations about what is appropriate in the specific situation. Any power move is also an implicit bid defining the relationships between those interacting. If you respond to the power move, you have confirmed its legitimacy. In this way, *power is confirmed through interaction*, often without being recognized by those involved.

WHAT ARE THE SOURCES OF POWER?

Because power springs from the willingness of others to endorse certain moves as appropriate, you should keep in mind that the most effective power tactics are the least obvious. Once we can recognize a power move, we can choose to withhold our endorsement. For this reason, power that is used in overt ways, such as rewards or punishments, tends to erode. Conversely, power based on defining issues is more difficult to challenge, and, therefore, more effective. In the following discussion, we examine different power sources and identify representative tactics.

Controlling the Terms and Grounds for Decision Making

Determining the power sources operating in any particular conflict is a complex process. Power can be employed in indirect ways or remain hidden beneath the surface of interaction. The most basic, hidden power source emerges through issue control. These power moves involve influencing the decision-making process by controlling whose concerns emerge as "problems" needing "solutions." Until Anita Hill's testimony during the Clarence Thomas confirmation hearings, for example, the issue of sexual harassment was frequently defined as a "nonissue," unworthy of serious attention.

If issues remain beneath the surface of interaction, it appears that no power is being used. As Bachrach and Baratz (1970) pointed out, however, power plays a vital role in suppressing issues that might threaten the values or interests of one of the parties in a conflict. "Nondecisions" and "nonevents" are actually the result of hidden power sources that go undetected.

Issue control is based on the power of the status quo or *habitual power*. It is usually easier to do things as they have always been done rather than change them. Habitual power discourages individuals from questioning the status quo—"But we've always done it this way. Why should we change it now?" The typical ways of doing things are considered to be "natural" and "neutral," making it difficult to raise alternative ideas.

Strong sanctions can result from violating unspoken norms about "how things are done around here." Despite a corporation's stated open-door policy that encourages employees to take their grievances to higher levels, an individual who does not follow the typical chain of command can experience a variety of punishments for challenging the issue control of their immediate supervisors. The fear of violating unspoken norms explains why even clear-cut cases of fraud and malfeasance are frequently suppressed rather than made explicit.

One way to assess hidden power dynamics is to look at effects. Ask yourself, "Whose interests are favored by the current definitions of organizational problems? Who determines the 'typical' procedures for making decisions?" Individuals who are consistently accommodated by others have habitual power. "Conservatives" who firmly oppose any change usually perceive a threat to their existing control of issues and procedures. They rely on the power of habits to prevent issues from emerging.

In addition, you should ask, "Who controls the *labels* attached to behavior?" Those who have the ability to define the terms of the dispute by attaching names to behavior have power. It makes quite a difference, for example, if the conflict is labeled a minor personality clash rather than a major dispute over basic principles. Many times, power is endorsed unconsciously by allowing one side to control the "terms of the debate." When you are involved in a conflict, think carefully about the language you use to describe the dispute—don't allow the other party to label the issues. Question their terms and insist on the use of your own language.

Finally, you can also recognize the tactics that are commonly used to deflect challenges to the status quo. *Refusal to recognize* that a conflict exists is a common tactic oriented toward maintaining issue control. Have you ever had a boss who responds to disagreements by saying, "I really don't think we disagree on this"? Refusing to acknowledge that differences are real and significant is an indirect tactic oriented toward coopting disagreement by defining it out of existence.

Postponement can function in a similar way. "I'm sorry, but we don't have time to talk about this issue now. Why don't you bring your concerns up at next month's staff meeting." If postponement is used consistently, it indicates issue control that is operating in the setting of group priorities. Postponement can be beneficial if key decision makers are not present or if the group needs a cooling-off period. All too often, however, organizations use postponement as a means of issue control—delay until the challengers become distracted by other issues, get tired, or move on to other jobs.

Issue expansion is a more direct tactic employed to counter challenges to issue control. One party purposely adds new issues to a conflict in order to direct attention away from the issue that threatens their interests. When the organization's fire and safety specialist identifies a number of serious safety violations on the shop floor, the shop foreman might try to direct attention away from the violations by shifting the issues, saying, "Well, that safety specialist clearly didn't read the memos I sent him explaining how we are using the shop equipment. My supervisor should have done a better job of following up on my memos."

Another variant of issue control is the use of an *umbrella* issue to legitimatize anger resulting from another issue. The marketing manager might feel that she has been slighted by the Accounting manager's comment, "You salespeople have it pretty easy. You get to entertain on company time." As the comment alone might not be a legitimate excuse to argue, the Marketing manager seizes instead on the Accounting department's tardiness in generating yearly expense summaries for individuals' taxes. The mistakes serve as the umbrella for the Marketing manager to take out her anger stemming from the thoughtless comment.

Gunnysacking, which is sometimes called injustice gathering, involves attacking by loading on a number of accusations at one time. The accuser dumps everything but the kitchen sink onto the target. A project team leader complains to the author of a report, "You've ruined our project report with your poor writing, sloppy spelling, and grammatical mistakes, and you were late, to boot! Your work is always sloppy. You can't even find things on your desk."

When the author of the report responds to only one part of the complaint, acknowledging, "Yes, the report was late," the gunnysacking tactic is being countered with a *fogging tactic*, which turns aside a criticism by only acknowledging a part of it. The other issues the accuser loaded on the target are ignored.

Fogging, gunnysacking, umbrella issues, and expanding the numbers of issues in a dispute are specific tactics that attempt to control the grounds and terms of the dispute. Postponement, refusing to acknowledge that a conflict exists, determining the criteria that will be applied to decision making, or having the ability to label the conflict are less visible. These tactics attempt to deflect competing priorities from emerging as serious topics for consideration. Because of their subtlety, many people overlook these hidden power sources.

Controlling Key Resources

Although attempts at issue control are frequently hidden or indirect, other power sources are more obvious. *Legitimate authority*

is power based on the privileges inherent in a particular job position. The ability to control important resources such as money,
equipment, or information typically comes with positions of
authority.

Threats and *promises* are tactics based on this source of
power. A threat involves the expressed intention to act in ways
that are detrimental to another, whereas a promise is an
expressed intention to act in beneficial ways. Although threats
and promises are usually backed by legitimate authority, you
need to do six things to make these tactics effective (Folger &
Poole, 1984).

First, ask yourself, "What is most important to the person
I am trying to influence? What do they value?" If an employee is
motivated by monetary rewards, a promotion will not lead to
superior performance unless the action includes an increase in
salary. On the other hand, an employee more concerned with status and esteem might find a bonus less rewarding than an
impressive title change. Effective rewards or punishments depend
on analyzing what different individuals value most highly. Don't
assume that everyone is motivated by the same things you are.

Second, determine how you can make your threats or
promises specific and vivid. A general statement such as, "Your
future depends on meeting this month's sales quota" will not be
as effective as the specific threat one retail regional manager
used with a store manager: "If you don't meet your sales quota by
the close of business on the 31st, I will personally show up at
your store at 9:00 a.m. the next morning to watch you clean out
your office."

A third factor is your credibility. You have to demonstrate
your ability to follow through. Are you really willing to do what
you have threatened? Can you deliver on the promised reward? If
you can't make your threats or promises "stick," you should use
other tactics.

Because of the credibility factor, rewards have an advantage over threats. In most instances, carrying through with a
reward tends to increase feelings of friendliness and trust, thereby increasing credibility. Using punishments, on the other hand,
can have the opposite effect.

Another factor affecting the effectiveness of a threat or
promise is its "immediacy." The more immediate you can make
the threat or promise, the more likely it is to be effective. You can
set specific time limits to make your rewards or threats more
immediate. Alternatively, you can provide a sample of the reward
or punishment.

A fifth factor influencing the effectiveness of a threat or promise is how those being influenced perceive it. Effective threats or promises are perceived to be fair, reasonable, justifiable, or beneficial (Kaplowitz, 1973). If those who you are attempting to influence do not perceive your threats or rewards to be fair in the specific context, they are more likely to resist your influence attempts. Terminating a user's e-Mail access if obscene messages are sent to another individual, for example, is likely to be perceived as an equitable response. Firing the offender could be perceived as unjust given the infraction. Your threats or promises must be tailored to the context.

Finally, you should analyze the group climate before using threats or promises. As we said in chapter 3, climate is the relatively enduring quality of group interaction that is experienced by group members as a whole. In competitive climates, for example, threats are perceived as attempts to coerce, whereas in cooperative climates threats are seen as attempts to influence the other for their own good (Folger & Poole, 1984). Your threats or promises must be perceived as being legitimate by others in the organization in order to be effective.

Rather than threaten directly, some individuals rely on a more indirect form of punishment—*nuisance power*. This tactic involves causing discomfort to another party without resorting to formal sanctions. Work-to-rule environments usually rely on nuisance power. In negotiating with the IRS, for example, you might employ nuisance power by submitting endless documentation in an effort to overwhelm the auditor with your supporting material. You might also insist on continual meetings to "clarify" what the issues are. Although nuisance tactics are frequently the refuge of the weak, this more indirect form of punishment can be used by those with formal authority as well.

A less tangible resource that can serve as the basis for power is information. *Information power* involves possessing information that is valuable to others. Other people's "need to know" permits the wielding of information power, as the insider trading cases of the 1980s illustrated. You can develop your information power by reading extensively, by joining task forces, by working on company-wide committees, or by attending conferences. The informal social connections between members of an organization are also important sources of information power—you don't need to be in a position of authority to develop it.

Negative inquiry is a specific tactic that relies on information power. When one party accuses or attacks, the target responds by asking for more information. If your manager claims that you have done an ineffective job, you might respond by asking for specifics. "What could I have done differently to avoid the problems you see?" This tactic, by clarifying issues, can expand the information level involved in decision making, and is a power resource that is open to all rather than just to those with formal authority. In chapter 2, we mentioned a number of other communication skills that you can use to clarify your perceptions.

Expert power stems from the special technical knowledge or unique skills that an organization needs to function. In a company like IBM, engineering and programming expertise are highly valued because of their connection to the core function of the organization. Expertise creates a dependency in the organization and develops in those jobs that are highly critical to the work flow. In such instances, expertise is a power source like information or control over rewards and punishments.

Your expert power will be enhanced if your expertise is in short supply, irreplaceable, and concentrated in the hands of a small number of people who cooperate. The air-traffic controllers who went on strike during the Reagan administration expected that their expertise would force management to negotiate. President Reagan illustrated, however, that the controllers could be replaced by military personnel, thereby devaluing the strikers' expertise power.

Appealing to Common Values

Another source of power is the ability to recognize and mobilize a group's common assumptions. As we have emphasized throughout this chapter, any power move must be confirmed by others in the organization. If you belittle a subordinate in public, you violate an unspoken rule that criticism should occur in a private setting that allows the target to save face. Ignoring this common assumption is likely to prompt direct challenges later on. Some forms of power are based more on intangible values than tangible resources.

Referent power, for example, develops if people admire or respect your moral, physical, or intellectual abilities. Those who are perceived as "having arrived" have referent power. Sometimes, those involved in "hot," "high profile" projects develop referent power because others admire their work. In some organizations, the person who has survived for the longest period of time develops referent power. Persuasive ability and likability can also serve as the basis for referent power. Unlike legitimate authority, which is based on a particular job description, referent power is based on your personal characteristics rather than your position in the hierarchy.

Positive or negative altercasting are specific tactics that play on our desire to be liked and respected by others. Positive altercasting involves telling one party in a dispute that "a wise" person would comply with the request. Negative altercasting associates "bad" qualities with those who do not comply. Telling someone that only a "petty" individual would object is an example of negative altercasting that relies on our desire to be respected by our peers.

Coalition formation is a another tactic that is based on common values. In this tactic, two or more parties form an alliance against another member. Baker (1981) found that the strongest influence prompting coalitions to form was the similar attitudes among members and that coalitions form around common goals and common enemies. We explained in chapter 3 how effective work teams can be powerful coalitions if they generate cooperatively structured goals. If you want to form a coalition, you should look first for agreement on important issues—the probabilities of success or obtaining a share of the payoffs were less important.

There are clearly a wide variety of power sources from which to draw, depending on the constraints you face. You can try to control what the "issues" are, you can try to control key resources such as information or rewards, or you can rely on appeals to common values. Effective managers use a variety of influence strategies, recognizing that what works in one situation might not be effective in another.

HOW DO TACTICS COMBINE INTO STRATEGIES?

Understanding power sources and tactics not only broadens your possible options, it helps you to anticipate the ebb and flow of moves and countermoves during conflict. By examining the types of power moves employed by others in a conflict interaction, you can learn a great deal about their intentions and their perceptions of their strengths and weaknesses (Folger & Poole, 1984). The power sources we draw on during conflict and the tactics we employ reveal our underlying conflict management strategies or styles.

Notice how the different power sources and tactics employed by the Chair Master and the violinists in the following case study illustrate complimentary styles. Attempting to exert the legitimate authority of his position, the Chair Master's accusations and threats indicate an assertive, controlling style. The violinists, on the other hand, form an alliance and attempt to avoid confrontation through tactics such as fogging and issue expansion.

Case Study 4.1: The First Violinists and The Chair Master

The Lewistown community orchestra was preparing for its upcoming Spring concert. The opening was only two weeks away and everyone was under a lot of stress. There was one piece in particular that was extremely difficult, and the Chair Master (best player) of the violinists set additional rehearsal time for the violinists. Two members of the section arrived 15 minutes late for the rehearsal and were unprepared. These two members were stand partners and close friends. The following dialogue took place between the two violinists and the Chair Master.

Chair Master: I can't believe that you would show up for rehearsal so blatantly unprepared. Are you trying to ruin the piece for everyone? Everyone here, excluding you, has spent weeks of practicing in preparation for this concert, and you walk in here and play like you've never seen the music before.

Violinist: We have been practicing, but this music is really difficult.

Chair Master: I am aware of your abilities, and you are not living up to them. You fool around during full orchestra rehearsals. You are both continually late, and now you show up to final rehearsals completely unprepared!

Violinist: It's true that we should have prepared more for practice.

Chair Master: I am going to have the conductor go down the line next week. If you still are unprepared, you will sit second violin section for the concert. Understood?

Violinist: Yes, we apologize for our lack of serious preparation.

The coalition of the violinists threatened the legitimate authority of the Chair Master. If two members of the section could flout the Chair Master's rules, others might well follow along, for power is confirmed through interaction, not position titles. The Chair Master attempted to seize issue control through applying negative labels to the violinists' behavior: "I can't believe you would show up for rehearsal so blatantly unprepared." Using negative altercasting, he asked, "Are you trying to ruin the piece for everyone?" Gunnysacking the tardy violinists, he reeled off numerous grievances and threatened the violinists with demotion. His threat was specific, immediate, and based on the violinists' interest in maintaining their position within the orchestra hierarchy.

The violinists attempt to deflect the Chair Master's verbal aggression by expanding the issues, complaining that the music is too hard. When that tactic doesn't work, they try fogging. They only acknowledge the Chair Master's complaint about poor preparation and they ignore his comments about tardiness and fooling around during rehearsals. When threatened with the loss of something they value—their standing within the orchestra—the violinists shift from avoiding to accommodating. Attempting to smooth over the differences, the violinists apologize for their lack of practice.

Individual power moves combine into sequences that reveal underlying conflict management strategies or styles. Although people's styles can, and often do, change during different stages of conflict interaction, it is helpful to understand your own preferences for conflict strategies. Do you try to avoid conflict, or do you tend to confront it head on?

Blake and Mouton (1964) identified five conflict-management strategies, asserting that people have relatively stable predispositions toward conflict strategies. More recently, researchers have questioned how consistent people are in using these styles. Communication scholars Ross and DeWine (1982), for example, have argued that rather than try to assess what people believe and feel about conflict, we should, instead, focus on what is said and done. By concentrating on the actual messages that you have used during a specific conflict episode, you can identify whether you focus on your own needs, the other's needs, or on the issue. The survey these researchers developed is included at the end of this chapter to help you identify the focus of your conflict messages.

Rather than view any one of these approaches as the best way to deal with conflict, you should look on them all as appropriate at different times depending on the conflict context. As we have suggested throughout this book, *effective conflict management requires flexibility*. In this section, we describe different conflict management strategies and identify when each might be appropriate.

Controlling

A controlling strategy, such as that of the Chair Master, relies on power or dominance to resolve a conflict, and reflects a psychological "fight" response to stress. A controlling orientation is a bid by the speaker for dominance in the interaction as typified by the following statements: "Can't you see how foolish you're being with that thinking?" or "You can't say that to me—it's either my way or forget it" (Ross & DeWine, 1982). Expressing an individual's need for control and lack of concern for the feelings of "the other," controlling statements convey an imperative to act immediately.

The downside to this method of conflict management is that the "losers" have no way to express their needs, and this can frequently create bigger problems. One of the authors worked as a trainee in a fast-food chain. During his training, he was told to order the supplies for the coming week even though he had not been trained in ordering procedures. When he tried to point this out to his superior, he was cut off and told to "Get with it and make the order!" Instead of ordering a week's supply of goods, he unknowingly ordered several months. The young manager trainee was blamed for placing the wrong order; however, his supervisor was also disciplined for his role in the fiasco.

However, controlling can be an appropriate method of conflict resolution if immediate action is required during a crisis, or if you feel you are right about a vital issue. When unpopular changes such as cutting budgets or firing personnel need to be implemented, a controlling strategy is usually required (Frank & Brownell, 1989). It can also be appropriate if this method has been agreed on by the group. Finally, some individuals take advantage of those they perceive to be "weak" or lacking in power. In dealing with such people, a forcing strategy is sometimes necessary, as the Chair Master seemed to assume.

Avoiding or Accommodating

A "flight" response is apparent in the *avoider* and *accommodator* strategies. In each approach, the differences between people are denied or "smoothed over"—individuals try to play down the extent of their differences and maintain surface harmony. These conflict-management strategies focus on the other more than the self or the issue. Statements such as, "I really don't have anymore to say on this . . . " or "That's O.K. . . . It wasn't important anyway" indicate an avoiding or smoothing strategy (Ross & DeWine, 1982).

When is *avoidance* appropriate? If an issue is trivial or more important matters are pressing, avoiding conflict can be an effective strategy. Sometimes people need a cooling-off period to gain perspective on the issues. Similarly, avoidance is appropriate if you are trying to gather information or feel that others could manage the conflict more effectively. You might avoid a conflict if you feel it is symptomatic of other problems. Avoidance, as we said in chapter 2, is also appropriate if you are being physically threatened. Finally, if you see no chance of satisfying your concerns, an avoidance strategy might be the best approach (Frank & Brownell, 1989).

Similarly, an *accommodating* strategy shows your flexibility if you find you are wrong or feel you are outmatched and need to retreat from your initial stance. By accommodating the concerns of others, you can build social credits for future use and help to develop group stability and cohesiveness. Finally, an accommodating strategy can be effective for allowing subordinates to develop by learning from their own mistakes (Frank & Brownell, 1989).

Over the long term, however, such strategies leave conflict issues to simmer under the surface to emerge indirectly in the form of defensiveness, resentment, or sabotage. Have you ever worked for a group that seemed cordial, friendly, and cooperative during staff meetings yet, behind the closed doors of their offices, they did nothing but complain about each other? Such an atmosphere can be a sign that avoidance and accommodating are being overused. We explained in chapter 3 more specific signs that indicate when avoidance is hampering decision making.

Compromising

Another conflict management strategy is the "I'll give in a little if you given in a little" approach. This is a *compromising strategy* characterized by statements such as, "Let's try finding an answer that will give us both some of what we want" (Ross & DeWine, 1982). Each side loses a little in order to compromise with the other party, resulting in a mixed outcome.

This method is appropriate if both parties have some latitude on the issue and are committed to mutually exclusive goals. It also is a less time-consuming strategy than collaboration, and is therefore frequently used by work units facing a limited time frame for decision making. Compromising yields temporary settlements of complex issues or serves as a backup when collaboration or force is unsuccessful.

Although we tend to think compromise is an effective con-flict-management strategy because it is the basis of our system of government, this approach, if overused, can have negative out-comes. The method encourages inflated initial positions that can be unrealistic. Rather than state "real" needs, each side exagger-ates their requirements in hopes of achieving more of their objec-tives during the process of "splitting the difference."

In terms of objective outcomes, a compromising strategy results in a solution that is watered down in order to balance each side's losses. The point of reference for decision making is internally located by the differences between each side. What gets lost in this process is a sense of what is happening outside of the organization (Anderson, 1993).

IBM's PC Junior computer was a classic example of how decisions based on compromise can fail to meet the market needs. This machine was the product of a compromise process between those in the company who argued for the importance of "smaller" computers and the "traditionalists," who favored main-frames and did not wish to see their large accounts cannibalized by efficient personal computers. The PC Junior, despite signifi-cant advertising support, was a resounding failure in the market-place. Decisions by compromise can create an internally focused organization that competes with itself rather than with its exter-nal business environment.

Compromise can also have negative effects on work rela-tionships. As we explain in detail in the next chapter, inflated starting positions have a tendency to develop into minimum requirements. One side may feel that they have given up a little more than the other and will expect the other side to do the same during the next conflict. Fisher and Brown (1988) argued that a good working relationship is not always based on reciprocity where a favor or concession by one side is expected for a similar favor or concession by the other. The "Golden Rule" is expedient, but it can produce outcomes based on inadequate information and poor analysis of options.

Collaborating

The collaborator strategy is characterized by a focus on mutual problem solving while maintaining interpersonal relationships. The abilities, values, and expertise of all are recognized, and the disputants work together to develop an integrative solution that merges insights from people with different perspectives. This approach focuses on building consensus about issues that are too important to be compromised and is characterized by statements such as, "I think we need to try to understand the problem" or "I'm really bothered by some things that are happening here; can we talk about these?" (Ross & DeWine, 1982). Collaboration builds commitment to solutions and fosters the learning process. For these reasons, this strategy is classified as a win/win conflict management style because each party is able to attain their individual goals.

Most scholars argue that collaboration is the most effective means of conflict management, but this method is time consuming and requires real commitment and skill on the part of those involved. In addition, collaboration requires a balance of power between disputants. All too frequently, these necessary conditions are not present in the conflict situation; thus, the most "effective" strategy for you depends on your diagnosis of the conflict context.

HOW DO EFFECTIVE MANAGERS USE POWER?

In many organizational disputes, you find yourself in conflict not with coequals, but with those above or below you in the organizational hierarchy. All too often, our assumptions about our power positions relative to others can skew our thinking in the conflict process. When you are attempting to influence others, you should try to avoid the "illusions" created by perceptions of strength as well as those generated by perceptions of weakness.

Avoiding the Dangers of Strength

Although being more powerful than the other side is usually seen as an advantage, this position can create its own dilemmas. Most immediately, any source of power tends to erode the more it is used. When power moves become obvious, people are more likely to withdraw their endorsement of that source of power.

A coerced employee may respond by reordering his or her values in such a way that punishments lose their sting and rewards are no longer alluring. In retrospect, the sanctions you threatened might appear less terrible than they seemed before they were actualized. An employee who is punished by being placed on the night shift might decide that they actually prefer that schedule as it provides them with the freedom to work with less supervision. Once people have lived through the consequences of a threat, it holds less power over them.

A second pitfall of strength is that the latitude for making exceptions becomes increasingly limited as you move up the organizational hierarchy. Those with legitimate authority are bound by the very procedures they have established to handle "normal" work situations. When confronted with the need to adapt to changing circumstances, such as conflict entails, the powerful can find themselves blocked by their procedures. In order to correct mistakes, those in a position of strength must overrule themselves. It thus becomes much more difficult for those in a position of strength to overcome their "trained incapacities."

The powerful need to recognize that conflict is a sign of change, and conflict episodes are frequently symptoms of underlying organizational problems. Before you assume that individuals are at fault, analyze the typical procedures established to handle "normal" work flows. Conflict episodes can be early-warning signs about practices that need to be adapted in the face of changing circumstances. Don't let a desire to save face by protecting the status quo take precedence over problem solving.

The powerful also often make false assumptions about the responses of the weaker party (Folger & Poole, 1984). The image the powerful create of the weak is one of a hostile or unfriendly adversary who will attempt to challenge any move. This imaginary conception of the opposition as being hostile can prompt you to take tougher stands to defend yourself against counterattack, regardless of the weaker person's actual feelings or intentions. An erroneous logic chain based on the projected fears of the stronger party can establish the grounds for destructive escalation cycles in which force and threats predominate. Don't project your fears onto the other side.

Conversely, if your influence attempts are successful, don't assume that agreement results from ingratiating behavior on the part of the weaker party rather than from your expertise and skill. All too often, powerful people assume that others change their minds out of fear rather than choice. Once your trust in the weaker party is undermined, it is difficult for you to recognize a willing change of mind among the weak.

Finally, don't underestimate the stamina of the weaker side. Because the stronger party can set the terms for reaching an agreement, the powerful might neglect to make de-escalation an attractive option. Give the weaker individual incentives to begin searching for a constructive solution. Don't create a situation in which the weak have nothing to lose by continuing with destructive behavior. "If the more powerful person demands total capitulation," Folger and Poole (1984) wrote, "continued fighting or avoidance of the issue might be more attractive to the weaker person than an attempt to resolve the conflict through negotiation or problem solving" (p. 138).

Avoiding the Dangers of Weakness

The dangers of weakness stem from the issue control that stronger parties can exert—thus, the needs of weaker members might not be seen as legitimate because the stronger party can often define what the conflict is about. Without input from the weak, the final solution can be ineffective or harmful because the group's grasp of the causes of the problem is incomplete.

Constructive conflict resolution requires that the definition of the problem incorporate the needs of *all* of the parties rather than favor the interests of the powerful. Recognize that we all participate in the renewal of power. If you are not persistent in withholding your endorsement of the stronger party's abilities to define the terms and the grounds of the conflict in their own favor, your issues will never emerge to become part of the final resolution. This means you must persistently question the issue control of the powerful.

Another danger of weakness is a tendency for the assumption of powerlessness to become a self-fulfilling prophecy. This perception can discourage you from attempting to exert influence or resist the countermoves of the powerful. Acts of desperation can occur when a member becomes so convinced of their own impotence they feel they have no recourse but to escalate the conflict in a desperate but doomed effort to turn the tide of the interaction. Look for alternative routes to power, and believe in your own abilities to be a fly in the ointment of the powerful.

In sum, effective managers are reasonably comfortable in using power to influence people. "They recognize that their attempts to establish power and use it are an absolutely necessary part of the successful fulfillment of their difficult managerial role" (Frank & Brownell, 1989, p. 430). In using their power, effective managers accept that they affect other people's professional lives in fundamental ways, but also recognize that power carries with it obligations to temper influence attempts with maturity and self-control. Effective managers seldom use their power to gratify their own egos—they realize that power used effectively tends to accumulate, while power used impulsively tends to erode.

So, if you are in-charge, there are a number of things you should keep in mind when attempting to influence others:

1. Know what motivates different individuals. Don't assume that everyone values the same things you do. Apply the communication skills we explained in chapter 2 to check your perceptions and clarify what others value.

2. Be sensitive to what others in your work unit and organization consider to be legitimate power moves. As we explained in chapter 3, the climate within a work unit sets a tone for interaction by encouraging the use of some tactics over others. Consider the impact your actions will have not just on an individual, but on the climate as a whole.

3. Be flexible and develop a variety of power sources beyond legitimate authority. Successful managers use a variety of tactics and adapt their strategies depending on the context, the individuals involved, and the issues.

4. Seek out positions that allow you to successfully develop and use power. Don't automatically avoid difficult assignments.

SUMMARY

Power dynamics shape our interactions in conflict situations, determining what we perceive as possible, necessary, and desirable. Recognize your own role in the renewal of power and develop a variety of power sources. You can try to control what the issues are, try to control key resources, or appeal to common values. Remember that obvious power moves based on unique power sources are easier to challenge than hidden power sources.

Vary your conflict management strategies depending on the context, the audience, and your own strengths and weaknesses. Avoiding, accommodating, controlling, compromising, and collaborating can all be effective in different situations. The key is to not fall into habitual responses. Finally, accept the responsibilities that come with power, balancing your influence attempts with judgement and maturity.

DISCUSSION QUESTIONS

1. Who has the formal authority in your organization? The informal? In what instances is one more "power-ful" than the other?
2. Has there ever been an attempt to challenge the habitual power in your organization? What happened? If not, are there any aspects of habitual power in your workplace that need changing?
3. What are the unspoken norms about how power is to used in your company?
4. What tactics are usually used by managers in your organization to deflect challenges to the status quo? Are they effective?
5. How is legitimate authority exercised in your organization?
6. Which do you feel is a more effective source of power: threats or rewards? Which are used more where you work? Are they effective?
7. How could you employ nuisance power in a recent negotiation and/or conflict?
8. Who has the information power in your organization? What would happen if this power source was eliminated?
9. Can you identify someone who has true referent power in your organization or local community? How did they attain this power?
10. What is your personal conflict management strategy? Has it been effective for you? Why or why not?

EXERCISES

Recall of Communication Behavior in Interpersonal Conflict (From Ross & Dewine, *Management Communication Quarterly*, *1*(3), pp. 410-411. Copyright © 1988 by Sage Publications, Inc. Reprinted by permission of Sage Publications, Inc.

Instructions
Consider situations in which you find yourself in conflict with another person. How do you usually respond in this situation?

1. List some of the ways you often behave, comments you frequently make, and feelings you often have, when you are in a conflict situation.

   _____

   _____

   _____

   Now, recall a *particular* conflict you have had with another person which is typical of the conflict situations you have described above.

2. What was the relationship of that person to you? Check the one that best describes the person:

   _____(1) Friend   _____ (5) Parent   _____ (9) Fellow Worker
   _____(2) Roommate _____ (6) Sibling   _____ (10) Employer
   _____(3) Boy/Girl   _____ (7) Child   _____ (11) Employee
         Friend   _____ (8) Stranger _____ (12) Other, Specify
   _____(4) Spouse

3. How close did you perceive the relationship to be at the time of the conflict? Check only one:

   _____(1) Very close
   _____(2) Close
   _____(3) Friends
   _____(4) Distant
   _____(5) Very distant

4. What was the conflict about?_____
   Talk about the conflict, yourself as a communicator in the conflict—how you behaved, things you remember saying, responses you made.

   _____

   _____

   _____

Conflict Management Message Style

Instruction

Listed below are messages delivered by persons in conflict situations. Consider each message separately and decide how closely this message resembles ones that you have used in conflict situations. *The language may not be exactly the same as yours, but consider the messages in term of similarity to your messages in conflict.*

There are no right or wrong answers. Keep in mind communicative behaviors described in the conflict recall. Answer in terms of the *responses you make*, not what you think you *should say*.

Give each message a 1-5 rating in the space provided according to the following scale. Use *one number only*.

In conflict situations, I:

1	2	3	4	5
never say things like this	rarely say things like this	sometimes say things like this	often say things like this	usually say things like this

1. _____ "Can't you see how foolish you're being with that thinking?"
2. _____ "How can I make you feel happy again?"
3. _____ "I'm really bothered by some things that are happening here; can we talk about these?"
4. _____ "I really don't have anymore to say on this . . . (silence). . . ."
5. _____ "What possible solutions can we come up with?"
6. _____ "I'm really sorry that your feelings are hurt—maybe you're right."
7. _____ "Let's talk this thing out and see how we can deal with this hassle."
8. _____ "Shut up! You are wrong! I don't want to hear any more of what you have to say."
9. _____ "It is your fault if I fail at this, and don't you ever expect any help from me when *you're* in a spot."
10. _____ "You can't do (say) that to me—it's either my way or forget it!"
11. _____ "Let's try finding an answer that will give us both some of what we want."
12. _____ "This is something we have to work out; we're always arguing about it."
13. _____ "Whatever makes you feel happiest is O.K. by me."
14. _____ "Let's just leave well enough alone."
15. _____ "That's O.K. . . . it wasn't important anyway. . . . You feeling O.K. now?"
16. _____ "If you're not going to cooperate, I'll just go to someone who will."
17. _____ "I think we need to try to understand the problem."
18. _____ "You might as well accept my decision; you can't do anything about it anyway."

Assessing Your Conflict Orientation—Scoring the Conflict Message Style
Survey

Record your answers to the questions in the following columns.
Total your score for each column.

Self	Issue	Other
1. ―――	3. ―――	2. ―――
8. ―――	5. ―――	4. ―――
9. ―――	7. ―――	6. ―――
10. ―――	11. ―――	13. ―――
16. ―――	12. ―――	14. ―――
18. ―――	17. ―――	15. ―――
Total ―――	Total ―――	Total ―――

REFERENCES

Anderson, J.W. (1993). On the razor's edge: Competing visions of organizational change. *The Pennsylvania Speech Communication Annual, 43*, 69-86.

Bachrach, P., & Baratz, M. (1970). *Power and poverty.* New York: Oxford University Press.

Baker, P.M. (1981). Social coalitions. *American Behavioral Scientist, 24*, 633-647.

Blake, R.R., & Mouton, J.S. (1964). *Solving costly organizational conflicts.* Houston, TX: Gulf.

Fisher, R., & Brown, S. (1989). *Getting together: Building relationships as we negotiate.* New York: Penguin.

Folger, J.P., & Poole, M.S. (1984). *Working through conflict: A communication perspective.* Glenview, IL: Scott, Foresman & Company.

Frank, A., & Brownell, J. (1989). *Organizational communication and behavior: Communicating to improve performance.* Orlando, FL: Holt, Rinehart & Winston.

Jamesway, E. (1981). *The powers of the weak.* New York: Morrow Quill.

Kaplowitz, S.A. (1973). An experimental test of a rationalistic theory of deterrence. *Journal of Conflict Resolution, 17,* 535-572.

Ross, R., & DeWine, S. (1982). *Interpersonal conflict: Measurement and validation.*

Tjosvold, D. (1985). Power and social context in superior-subordinate interaction. *Organizational Behavior and Human Decision Processes, 35*(3), 281-293.

▶ 5

Negotiating Agreements

INTRODUCTION

In this chapter, we look at power moves in action by focusing on negotiation. Although we tend to associate negotiation with collective bargaining in which representatives for labor and management hammer out formal work contracts, this method of conflict resolution is widely used in organizations. Managers negotiate raises with their employees or bargain with suppliers over the cost of materials. Every time you buy a car or a house, you engage in a negotiation process—it is one of the most common formal techniques for creating agreements in the workplace.

To explain the basics of negotiating, we begin by describing the negotiation context. We then consider some of the common obstacles to negotiating and discuss the importance of planning in the process. Next, we examine the phases through which many negotiations progress and provide suggestions for balancing competition with collaboration. Finally, we conclude by summarizing the characteristics of effective negotiators and negotiation processes.

WHAT IS NEGOTIATION?

"Negotiation," Putnam (1985) asserted, "represents a particular type of conflict management—one characterized by an exchange of proposals and counterproposals as a means of reaching a satisfactory settlement" (p. 129). What distinguishes this method of conflict management is the fact that communication is more consciously controlled than in other conflict situations (Putnam & Roloff, 1992). The exchange of proposals and counterproposals defines differences more clearly than other methods of conflict management, in which differences can remain diffused or suppressed. Negotiation takes place with a knowledge of existing factions and power differentials, making conflict tangible and explicit—many people are intimidated by this clarification of incompatibilities. As Leeson and Johnston (1988) pointed out, negotiation "is . . . a psychological confrontation" (p. 103). Successful negotiators approach this psychological confrontation with confidence.

Although negotiation involves more controlled communication than other conflict situations, the overall process is marked by greater ambiguity because our lack of control over the outcome is clearly apparent at the onset. How can we get the "other" to do what they would not normally want to do? The process of "give and take" is so contingent on the responses of the other side that certainty is impossible. Effective negotiators tolerate the ambiguity in the process and do not allow it to intimidate them. It helps, however, to have an idea of some of the common pitfalls that plague many negotiations.

WHAT ARE THE OBSTACLES TO EFFECTIVE NEGOTIATION?

Negotiation is only possible when both sides have the desire and the capability to reach an agreement. In order to be successful, you need to be able to identify when negotiation is possible, who to negotiate with, and how to avoid biases in your own thinking. Successful negotiators have a clear sense of their own needs and interests as well as a good intuitive understanding of the other side. They avoid certain common pitfalls.

Obstacles Presented by the Other Side

In some negotiation situations, agreement is not the goal of the other side. They might be interested in stalling for time, making points with their constituents, or obtaining media coverage for their grievances. Both sides must be interested in reaching an agreement through negotiation in order for the process to yield productive results.

If both parties are not committed to reaching an agreement, negotiations are likely to become bogged down in technicalities. During the 1955-1956 Montgomery Bus Boycott negotiations, for example, the representatives for the city were not really concerned with hiring black drivers and organizing seating on the buses (Mier & Gills, 1992). The city officials were only interested in finding a means to return to the status quo. The Montgomery boycott continued until the U.S. Supreme Court ruled Alabama's state and local laws unconstitutional.

In many instances, coercive power is necessary in order to get the parties motivated to negotiate. The bus boycott employed economic force to demonstrate the importance of African Americans to the municipal services of the city, and, more broadly, to the nation as a whole. Ultimately, though, the force of federal law enforcement was necessary. Most commonly, the less powerful attempt to use coalition power to motivate the more powerful to talk. Labor unions use strikes to get management to agree to talk. A lockout by management of the workers illustrates that the workers are not vital to the functioning of the organization. These forcing techniques are used to establish the basic conditions necessary for negotiation. You should try to avoid negotiating with those who are not committed to reaching agreement through the process.

A second common obstacle to effective negotiation involves negotiating with those who do not have the power to reach an agreement. Unless you are negotiating with someone who has the authority to make a valid commitment, you are placing yourself at a disadvantage. Car dealers use this tactic all the time to obtain a second bite of the apple. You negotiate the best price that you can with the car salesperson who then says, "Well, I'll have to check this out with my sales manager." The salesperson then returns with a higher figure than agreed on. Unless you negotiate with the real decision maker, your efforts will be whittled down by each intermediary level. The other side has an opportunity to negotiate again, causing you to lose ground.

In such instances, you should treat all agreements as tentative. If they demand another round of negotiations, so should you: "Let's treat this agreement as tentative. You check this out with your sales manager, and I'll go to the Acura dealer down the street and see what they can do." Don't allow the other side to reopen negotiations.

Obstacles From Your Side: Perceptual Biases

Experimental gaming and behavioral decision theory provide useful insights into why negotiators sometimes behave irrationally. Common perceptual biases can skew the negotiation process, leading to "systematic deviations from rationality that a negotiator can expect from his or her own behavior" (Neale & Bazerman, 1991, p. 41). The way bargaining issues are framed, the target and reservation points we set, and the ways in which we process information can all bias our thinking during the negotiation process.

The first factor that influences our negotiating behavior is the way in which the issues under dispute are framed. In framing an issue we are defining a perspective, directing attention toward the figure or the background in the same stimulus. A negative frame casts issues in terms of losses (i.e., lives lost), while a positive frame casts issues in terms of gains (lives saved).

Neale and Bazerman (1985) found that "negatively framed negotiators were less concessionary and reached fewer agreements than positively framed negotiators. In addition, negotiators who had positive frames perceived the negotiated outcomes as more fair than those who had negative frames" (p. 45). The frame or the context in which the issues are placed creates different expectations about outcomes and thereby influences the type of negotiating strategies we choose.

When looking at potential gains, individuals are risk-adverse, selecting conservative strategies. In negotiation, risk avoidance translates into accepting an offered settlement. When confronted with potential losses, on the other hand, individuals become risk seekers; they hold out for more concessions and are less willing to accept offered settlements. We suggest that in order to induce cooperation in your opponents, you should cast issues in positive terms of the other's potential gains. As we mentioned in discussing the dilemmas of weakness and strength, if people perceive that they have nothing to gain from negotiating, they can decide to pursue risky and destructive strategies.

Another factor that can bias a negotiation process is confusing target points with reservation points. A target point defines the ideal, the best possible outcome you could hope to achieve. Your reservation point, in contrast, is the point at which you walk away from the table, accepting no agreement rather than an agreement that does not meet your minimum requirements. Although high target points set the parameters of the negotiation, they can also lead to a stalemate by establishing a negative frame for the negotiation. The distinction between the "ideal" and the "actual" is lost as each side sees losses rather than gains and becomes risk-seeking rather than risk-adverse (Roloff & Jordon, 1989).

The way we store and retrieve information from memory also influences our judgements in the negotiation process. Although negotiators use past experience as a guide, not all events are coded in memory in an easily accessible manner. In a series of experiments, respondents heard a list of well-known personalities of both sexes and were asked to determine whether the list contained more men than women. In one group, the women were more recognizable than the men, but there were more men on the list. In the other group, the men were more well-known than the women, but there were more women on the list. Subjects incorrectly guessed that the sex of the more famous personalities were more numerous (Neale & Bazerman, 1991).

When you judge the frequency of an event, those events that are more easily recalled will seem more numerous to you. In other words, you are likely to overestimate unlikely events that you remember clearly. A violent outburst, for example, will be remembered because of its vividness. The likelihood of another such incident will be overestimated because it is easily remembered.

Despite these persistent perceptual biases, many decision-makers are overly confident in their judgment abilities. Ironically, questions of moderate to extreme difficulty prompt the most overconfidence (Fishchoff, Slovic, & Lichtenstein, 1977; Korait, Lichtenstein, & Fishchoff, 1980). When overconfidence occurs, the target points become more extreme, reducing the incentive to compromise.

There are additional factors that can skew our decision making. Small sample sizes will not demonstrate the characteristics of bigger ones, but people typically ignore the role of sample size in assessing the validity of new information. Selective perception plays a role in biasing our judgments because we only pay attention to evidence that supports our preconceived ideas.

Finally, our judgments of causation can influence our expectations. Interpersonal research indicates that we typically attribute positive outcomes to our own behavior, while negative outcomes are attributed to environmental factors that are beyond our control. In judging our own behaviors, we tend to overestimate our cooperativeness while overestimating the other side's competitiveness. Such causal accounts are important because they shape our expectations about future events. As we said in chapter 4, don't project your fears onto the other side; instead, strive to understand their needs in their own terms.

HOW CAN YOU PLAN FOR THE NEGOTIATION?

Once you have determined if the necessary preconditions exist for negotiating, you should look carefully at your own needs and interests. Planning is key to successful negotiations. Negotiators who define specific, quantifiable goals to which they remain committed do better than negotiators who do not have specific expectations about outcomes (Roloff & Jordon, 1992). Clear, specific goals are crucial because they establish the anchor points for discussion. "People estimate values for unknown objects or events by starting from an initial anchor value and adjusting from there," Neale and Bazerman (1991) explained: "Once negotiators respond to these demands with suggested adjustments, this act gives credibility to that anchor" (p. 48). Research has shown that final agreements are more strongly influenced by initial offers than by subsequent concessionary behavior (Liebert, Smith, Hill, & Keiffer, 1968; Yukl, 1974).

For this reason, a tough-to-soft strategy is more effective than the reverse because it takes advantage of the anchoring effect of high initial offers. The "reformed sinner" strategy, in which one party initially competes then turns to cooperation, is an attempt to avoid the negative frame that can develop as a result of high initial demands. While clear, specific, and moderately difficult goals are crucial to the negotiation process, you must be realistic in setting them. If your goals are grossly inflated, you run the risk of creating a negative frame for the process. Your opening demands should not create the impression that you are not interested in coming to an agreement through negotiation.

Although it is very unlikely that the negotiation will develop as you planned, having a clear sense of your own goals will keep you focused throughout the process. Folger, Poole, and Stutman (1993) suggested asking the following questions:

- What do I think are the main issues in this negotiation?
- What does the other party think are the main issues in this conflict?
- What are my requirements for a successful resolution?
- What is my best possible outcome? What is the least I can accept?
- What are the other party's needs and requirements for a successful resolution?
- What are some possible solutions that would meet my needs?
- What solutions would meet both of your needs?
- How do I feel about this matter?

Having tough but realistic goals, staying focused on those goals, and being confident about your abilities are the hallmarks of successful negotiators. Again, although planning is important, you should be committed to your goals but flexible about the means for fulfilling them. In the actual negotiation, events are not likely to progress as you planned.

WHAT CAN YOU EXPECT DURING THE NEGOTIATION?

Understanding negotiation phases can also help you deal with the uncertainty in the process. By recognizing the different actions that are necessary to create an agreement, you can understand the focus of activity at a given time and anticipate what might come next. Holmes (1992) defined negotiation phases as "coherent periods of activity that center on a particular subgoal or milestone in the negotiation" (p. 86).

There are a variety of different labels for the stages of negotiation depending on the preferences of the researcher. Most models, however, identify at least three broad phases: initiation, problem solving, and resolution. Unsuccessful negotiations tend to get stalled in an intermediate phase or bounce between early phases.

In order to illustrate negotiation phases, we will use an extended case study. The participants in this simulation were taking part in a negotiation training program in which their tasks were to decide among three different versions of a house to build (Madison, Columbia, or Richmond); to agree on a purchase price, including options; and to agree on a move-in date. You will notice that this negotiation does not progress neatly through each of the three stages. This example does, however, allow us to illustrate different behaviors that mark different periods of the interaction.

Initiation Phase

The *initiation phase* of negotiation focuses on discovering incompatible goals and defining multiple issues. Each party attempts to specify priorities and clarify differences. "The style is one of forensic fireworks" as vehement demands are made (Holmes, 1992, p. 88).

Although issues are important, there is another, more subtle, negotiation occurring during this phase. What type of relationship will develop between the parties? All negotiations take place on two levels—issues and relationships. The challenge of the initiation phase is to clarify differences on issues without creating a negative frame that breaks the relationship between the parties. In the following case study, notice how each side tests the strength of the other side by asking skeptical questions.

Case Study 5.1: The New House Negotiation—Initiation

Sellers: *Congratulations on your choice of River Knolls. We look forward to selling you one of our beautiful houses overlooking the scenic Hudson River. We hope we can come to a win/win agreement.*
(Nervous laughter from the buyers).
Buyers: *Congratulations to you. You're, uh, ready to sell (nervous laughter) a house in a period when business isn't that great and we hope we can help you out.*
(Discussion about what the buyers do for a living)
Sellers: *We've been around for so long that we have really good contacts, excellent equipment, contractors, and wholesalers, so we do a really nice job as far as the construction of the house and materials that we use.*
Buyers: *So, what type of materials do you use? Are the houses well insulated?*

Sellers: Oh, of course. All of our houses are well insulated. I mean, you're not looking at a house in Myrtle Beach.

Buyers: So, what type do you use?

Sellers: All of our houses have the Standard Energy Package. You want to know the brand name?. . .

Buyers: Let's talk about the houses you're offering us. Can you tell us what the basic differences are?

Sellers: All three houses can be tailored to your needs. It depends what you're looking for. Do you need a very large space for your work? I believe the Madison's the largest if you're looking for size.

Buyers: We do a lot of work out of the home, so size is important. Resale value is also important.

Sellers: That's always an important thing that we try to stress to people. The options we offer improve the resale value of our homes. You can even adapt the basements in the Richmond and Columbia model to accommodate apartments. That's a really smart option to look into because when you're selling it's an easier thing to resell because of the larger space.

Buyers: That's against the zoning codes.

Sellers: We're not the law. I'm not going to tell you to do something, but I know when I bought my house the real estate agent told me the same thing—"Other people do it, go ahead" . . .

Buyers: The Madison already has the extra square footage.

Sellers: Yeah, the Madison is a larger house, but it doesn't have the option to add a separate apartment.

Buyers: Well, since we're interested in size, it seems the Madison would be what we're looking for. Let's talk about the prices you're asking.

Sellers: The base price on the Madison is $123,900.

Buyers: That's taking into account the market? The prices seem pretty high.

Sellers: No. . . . Not at all. We've got river-view property. We've got a top-notch reputation. There's nothing comparable to the quality of our homes.

Buyers: Let's talk about some of the other houses on the market. (They pull out listings of other houses). Here's a house for $66 per square foot with a marble entry, master bedroom suite, whirlpool . . .

Sellers: What size house is this?

Buyers: 3,000 square feet

Sellers: In what location?

Buyers: In this area.

Sellers: That's not a new house, obviously.

Buyers: They're brand new houses.

Sellers: That house is listing for $200,000. Do you have that kind of money to spend?

Buyers: You're asking $83 per square foot. We're just saying that someone in the area is asking $66-$79 and that for you to come down a bit on the base price would not be outrageous.

Sellers: It's a fact that most of our costs are in fixed expenses such as the land and the labor to construct these houses. Our houses target a different buyer, a first-time home buyer.

Buyers: We're just saying it's not unreasonable for you to come down a little bit. What do you think about that?

Sellers: Well, we're willing to be flexible. We can't just jump into the price. We have to talk about the house options. What options do you want to include?

Buyers: We definitely want the Madison, and depending on what we get for a base price, we can decide what options we can get. We have to see what you can do with the base.

Sellers: Well, we're not willing to negotiate on the base price without talking about options.

Buyers: Well, we're not going to have an idea of what we can afford to buy without knowing the base price.

Sellers: Did you have a base price you were looking to work with?

Buyers: Our assessment of the market indicates there's pretty much a 20% reduction. Reduction is normal in the market today because the market is so glutted.
(Silence from the sellers).

Buyers: Even with the 20% reduction in current market prices, your prices are 20% over the market so we should be offering you 40% lower.

Sellers: I'm really hesitant to talk about the base price of the house before we talk about what's going into the house itself.

Buyers: It's not like we're going to take the base without any options. We're just saying that the market assessment is basically 20% off the asking price.

Sellers: O.K., you have to look at this also. You're buying your first house, and you want to come out well, but we have to make a profit, too. Asking us to come down 20% means we'll walk away with almost nothing.

Buyers: *How much can you come down?*

Sellers: *What we're saying is we can't even assess how much we can come down on our base price until we have some kind of idea if you're looking into getting any kind of options. It works out both ways, you know.*

Buyers: *Obviously we want options. . . . As a matter of fact, we want a lot of options, but we don't know what we're going to be able to afford. You know what I'm saying?*

Sellers: *O.K. I understand where you're coming from. The thing is, it's hard for us to have an idea of how much leeway we can give. We're not trying to take you for all your money. We want to make a profit just like you want to come out with something you're comfortable with. I understand that.*

In terms of content, initiation phases are marked by the proliferation of issues. During this stage, issues multiply and become subdivided. Each party evaluates the strengths and weaknesses of the other side and prioritizes issues differently. The discussion in the initiation phase may seem confusing as each side tries to discover the priorities of the other.

In this case, the minor issues such as building materials, insulation, and zoning laws served as a cover for negotiating the relationships. The buyers, by relying on negative inquiry, indicated their distrust of the sellers. The sellers responded by focusing on their overall trustworthiness and questioning the buyers about the money they had to spend. The early interaction in this negotiation revolved around defining the nature of the relationships between the parties. How tough is the other side? How much can they be trusted?

At this stage of the negotiation, it is important to look behind the issues to ascertain the interests that motivate the positions. Fisher and Ury (1981) clarified the difference between *interests* and *positions*. "The basic problem in a negotiation lies not in conflicting positions, but in the conflict between each side's needs, desires, concerns, and fears" (p. 42). Your position is something you decide on; your interests are what caused you to take this stand.

Often, it is our different interests that provide the basis for collaborative solutions. In this case, the buyers were concerned with the overall cost per square foot of the house they were buying. They had a limited amount of money they could spend. The sellers, on the other hand, had an interest in selling options as well as the house. They made a higher profit percentage on the options than they did on the base price.

A way to determine people's interests is to ask them why they want their positions. The sellers consistently probed to discover what motivated the buyers. By shifting topics and asking questions, the sellers searched for the interests of the other side. In addition to asking why, Fisher and Ury (1981) suggested that you should also ask, "Why not?" (p. 44). "Why not the Richmond or the Columbia?" Remember that each side has multiple interests and that the challenge of the initiation phase is to get these interests on the table without falling into escalation cycles.

Consequently, you should be prepared to talk about your interests and make them specific. Rather than reacting emotionally to the buyers' tough stance on the base price, the sellers responded by describing their need to discuss options before making concessions on the base price. While you should avoid labeling or accusing the other side (i,e., "That's outrageous!"), don't be afraid to describe your reactions to the other person's actions ("To ask us to come down 20% will mean we'll walk away with almost nothing"). You can't expect the other side to be mind readers. Help the other person understand how their actions affect you.

Although you do want take advantage of the anchoring effect of demanding initial offers, you want to avoid being unreasonable. In this example, the buyers risked escalating the conflict when they offered a price 40% below the listing price. This offer removed *any* profit for the sellers. Stalemate was avoided because the sellers focused their comments on behaviors, not on psychological states or personality traits. The sellers refused to respond to the unreasonable demand and shifted the conversation to their interest in knowing what options the buyers wanted.

Successful initiation phases avoid stalemate while getting the range of different interests on the table. Conversely, unsuccessful initiation phases result when the parties engage in attack-defend cycles. Matching statements of one's opponents leads to a tighter interaction pattern that can spark escalation. Successful negotiations are marked by flexibility of behaviors. The parties do not mirror the other sides' behavior, nor do they rely on a mechanical splitting of the difference without ascertaining the range of issues. Topic shifting helped this group avoid deadlock while identifying each side's different interests.

In sum, you should expect issues to multiply in this initial phase of negotiation. Recognize, however, that some issues serve as the cover for negotiating relationships. Don't mirror the actions of the other side, but probe for the interests that lie behind positions. Be prepared to talk about your needs and make them specific. The challenge of this initial phase of negotiation is to clarify differences in a way that does not break the relationship between the parties or lead to escalation cycles.

Problem-Solving Phase

During the *problem-solving phase*, the conversation shifts from asserting priorities to talk focusing on problem solving. The function of the problem-solving stage is to sift through, reduce, and jointly evaluate the multiple issues raised in the first stage. This phase is characterized by reason-giving behavior, information exchange, and bartering. Negotiators may withdraw issues, accent or sharpen others, transform issues through redefinition, or add facts and interpretations to refocus issues. Through this phase, negotiators look for areas of agreement that are promising, but will make concessions reluctantly only after clear signs of tacit agreement.

Case Study 5.2: The New House Negotiation—Circling Toward Problem Solving

Buyers: Let's say we offered you $89,000 for the base then add the options on top of that. Is that reasonable?

Sellers: I can tell you that $89,000 is just . . . is nowhere near something we can work with.

Buyers: Can't you give us one figure?

Sellers: O.K., wait a second. Now I'm not saying we can't work something out on the Madison. I'm sure we can. Can you give me one second? . . . The options we can work with a lot more than our base price. You know what I'm saying?

Buyers: I see where you're coming from, but I don't think our offer is unreasonable since we have these estimates on other houses. I think we've found a middle ground looking at the market percentage wise. I don't think that's an unreasonable figure because your prices seem overinflated compared to others.

Sellers: 20% . . . Our homes are not overinflated by 20%.

Buyers: Well, what do you feel is not . . .

Sellers: We don't feel the house prices are overinflated, but there's a point we can negotiate on.

Buyers: Well, can you give us an idea of what that would be?

Sellers: All right. . . . I need a little more information. Are you looking at moving in at a certain time? We have a Richmond model or a Columbia model that will be ready by the end of December. We don't currently have a Madison model under construction so it will take longer. When do you need to move?

Buyers: Why should that make a difference?

Sellers: We need to plan our construction schedule and things like that. When do you need to move in by?

Buyers: We're escalating. . .

Sellers: Exactly. . . . Let's take a step back. We just need to know when you want to move in. . . . We need a date— do you have a specific date? Like February first?

Buyers: Uhm, hmm . . . (The buyers confer among themselves) Fine. We can live with that.

Sellers: How would you feel about taking a break?

Buyers: Yeah. . . . That sound like a good idea. (Side-bar conferences)

Buyers: We've decided on the Madison.

Sellers: O.K.

Buyers: So right now we're negotiating on a base price and based on that we can figure out what options we can negotiate on.

Sellers: Right.

Buyers: And we want to have a number of options, but we won't be able to tell how many we can actually afford until we know that. I think we want to hear what you think is a fair price.

Sellers: Right now the base price on the Madison is $83. per square foot, right? O.K., we're willing to come down to $79 per square foot. That will bring the base price down to $117,000.

Buyers: Well, you've just said you make your profit on options. . . . Don't you think it would be in your best interest to come down?

Sellers: This is just out of control. We don't make that much.

Buyers: Well, you know what? We had discussed the base and we realized that $89,000 is low. A 20% discount is really $99,000.

Sellers: O.K., you asked us how far we can come down with what we know about now. We gave you a price. We need to talk about options first. We're not coming into anything with out talking about options. . . . You're going to talk about options you want before we talk fur-

ther about base price.

Buyers: *We'll give you a list of options, but we don't really want to discuss option prices yet.*

Sellers: *All right, no problem.*

Buyers: *On these larger options, like additional bathrooms, that's really going to have a lot to do with us getting the base price down.*

Sellers: *Let's not even speak in dollars. What is it you'd like to have? Just say you had a thousand million dollars or whatever. . . .*
(General laughter)

Buyers: *We definitely want another bathroom. We're gonna need a dishwasher and all the appliances.*

Sellers: *Great, we have a good appliance package.*

Buyers: *And we need an additional back door.*

Sellers: *It's an option that's a necessity.*

Buyers: *The sink with a garbage disposal. Now looking at the types of things we want, what kind of a deal . . . How far can you come down on the base? We're not going to be able to afford all these things without some change on that.*

Sellers: *We know where you're coming from. Let me just . . . Lower level exterior door, an absolute for that. An absolute with all your appliances, correct? O.K., you'd like to have another bathroom but you need to work something out so that you're not taking the base price and adding on $20,000 worth of options, correct?*

Buyers: *Correct. As you can see, we're not being chintzy on the options.*

Sellers: *We understand that.*

Buyers: *We do realize you have to act in your best interests too.*

Sellers: *O.K. Give us about five minutes so we can discuss this for a second.*
(Sellers confer, while buyers chat)

The critical task in the problem-solving phase is the shifting, reducing, and joint evaluation of multiple issues. Dropping minor objections and simplifying complex issues contributes to generating agreements. During this phase you should try to define problems in the smallest terms, for this will make them easier to resolve. Fractionate the problem, separating it into manageable levels.

Movement toward problem solving begins when one party makes a real counteroffer rather than sticking to their ideal preference. In this case, the first agreement came on a relatively minor issue—the move-in date. After the buyers' first concession, the sellers responded with a 5% reduction on the purchase price. Frequently, agreement can be found more easily on minor issues. Such small agreements help create a climate of cooperation rather than competition.

Although dropping many subissues, the buyers maintained a focus on a 20% reduction in the base price. In relying on an objective standard generated by the marketplace, the buyers employed one of the standard tactics of principled negotiation. Fisher and Ury (1981) argued that insisting on objective criteria is a helpful technique during the problem-solving phase. Criteria may be thought of as guidelines for defining what is a fair solution. Without identifying objective criteria, it may be difficult to determine when a solution is reached.

Insisting on agreement over objective criteria depersonalizes the decision-making process, grounding it in something other than subjective feelings. By using the market to generate an objective standard, the buyers made their request for a significant reduction in the base price appear reasonable. Throughout the process, the group's focus on the cost per square foot kept their thinking anchored in reality. When they bartered, it was over a standard that was related to reality. In this way, they avoided the problems that can come from a mechanical splitting of the difference that anchors decision making in internal dynamics that ignore the external environment.

When objective criteria can't be decided on, you might try such procedures as one side cuts, the other chooses. You can try taking turns in who selects first. You can rely on flipping a coin, or having a third party decide. Such techniques are less effective than objective criteria, but they might help you invent options for mutual gain.

Settlement on the central issue of money in our case study grew from a creative packaging of the issues. A package deal emerged in which the buyers agreed to options and the sellers agreed to reduce the base price. Through the problem-solving stage, the parties developed a tacit agreement on relating agreement on purchasing options to agreeing to reduce the base price.

Resolution Phase

The third phase, *resolution*, usually occurs as deadlines approach. This phase is characterized by formalizing agreements and attending to the details of the final agreement. Clear and precise language is crucial for an effective, durable agreement. Douglas (1962) found that three strategies facilitated the narrowing of options at this point. A yes-no format of question and answers aided the careful control of information. Forced-choice options also helped the narrowing process, as did side-bar conferences alternating with official meetings.

Case Study 5.3: Resolving the New House Negotiation

Sellers: *Do you guys have . . . do you have a, uhm, maximum amount you can spend? Because we're trying to work this out for you. What price are you looking at now?*

Buyers: *Why don't you give us an idea of the figure you are looking at.*

Sellers: *All right. We're looking at the lower level door, and your appliances. . . . The base we have down to $117,900.*

Buyers: *We need that lower. 'Cause we want those options.*

Sellers: *We're already coming down $6,000 on our base price of the house.*

Buyers: *So you are coming down 5%? Do I have that right? You've got to come down closer to 20%. . . . At least to 15%.*

Sellers: *We can't do 15. We can do 12. . . . O.K., we need to discuss the bathroom for a second. Are you looking at a basic bathroom or are you looking for custom-made cabinets and a deluxe bathtub.*

Buyers. *We're looking for something that functions.*

Sellers: *O.K. and all appliances included, the dishwasher, the washer/dryer, refrigerator, and we'll throw in the garbage disposal and hot water tap, O.K. . . . An additional bathroom and fireplace would come too. These options come to $12,000. We can go down on the price of the house. We can go down to 10% off the base price. Is that what you said?*

Buyers: *Twelve.*

Sellers: *Twelve. We'll go down to 12% off the base with $12,000 in options. That brings the total price down to $121, 032. And that's still a few thousand dollars less*

> *than the original base price of the house.*
> *Buyers: Can you give us a second? (They start to discuss the*
> *package among themselves).*
> *Sellers: This deal is a real steal.*
> *Buyers: I have it coming closer to $81. per square foot. With*
> *12% off the base, that comes to $109,000. That's closer*
> *to what it should've been to begin with.*
> *Sellers: We don't feel that way at all.*
> *Buyers: How much did you come down on the options, just out*
> *of curiosity?*
> *Sellers: We came down a thousand . . . two thousand.*
> *Buyers: The market reduction is closer to 20%.*
> *Sellers. Well, then, we'll just have to relook at that 12% then,*
> *because that's the only way the package works for us.*
> *That's the same price we're selling our smaller models*
> *for.*
> *Buyers: How much are you charging us for the bathroom? And*
> *the lower level door? What happens if we come down*
> *10% on that?*
> *Sellers: We came down even more than we planned.*
> *Buyers: We need a listing of the prices on the options.*
> *Sellers: O.K. we're doing that right now. Hang on one second. . . .*
> *I just gotta make sure. . . . O.K. we're looking at a price of*
> *$121,032.*
> *Buyers: $121,000. Wow, we're all happy about this.*
> *Sellers: Shall we shake hands on it?*

Inventing options for mutual gain developed by determining the different interests implicit in the negotiation. Discovering the interests behind stated positions facilitated the creative problem-solving process by broadening the range of potential resources that can form a part of the final resolution. The parties in this negotiation came to a win/win agreement through packaging issues together. The sellers came close to their profit targets by selling more profitable options, while the buyers gained amenities and came close to their target point in base price. The different interests made a creative agreement, meeting the needs of both sides.

By the end of this process, the parties had moved from competition to collaboration as the frame for the negotiation moved from negative to positive. Each side saw gains in their package deal. When the buyers tried to reopen negotiations on the option prices, the sellers threatened to reopen the negotiations on the base price. Faced with losing their gains on the base price, the buyers became risk-adverse, retreating from their attempt to reopen negotiations. Attack-defend cycles became shorter and did not escalate out of control.

The use of forced-choice answers facilitated the resolution process by reinforcing the tentative agreements the buyers had made on options: "An absolute for all your appliances, correct?" These forced-choice questions narrowed the range of options under consideration and confirmed agreements in a way that made it difficult to withdraw from at a later date. This technique helped break a complex agreement into smaller, manageable agreements.

Lewicki and Litterer (1985) offered additional suggestions for inventing options for mutual gain. *Expanding the pie* is a technique in which scarce resources are altered to produce gains for each individual. In one negotiation group, the buyers agreed to allow the sellers to use their house as a model for six months to sell other prospective buyers. Sometimes it helps to separate, temporally and physically, the act of creating options from the process of evaluating them. This means you must be prepared to use setting and timing creatively to facilitate creative thinking.

Another technique is to pay off one party with some other form of compensation, known as *nonspecific compensation.* One side attempts to discover what is valued by the other party, and this is used to "pay them off" for what they do not get in the negotiation. Employee A may want to use the copy machine, but employee B has been given the use of the machine at the time employee A wants to use it. Employee A may be told that if he lets employee B use the copy machine at his desired time, he will be compensated with extra overtime at a later date. Obviously, nonspecific compensation requires trust among the parties involved.

HOW CAN YOU BALANCE COMPETITION WITH COLLABORATION?

Successful negotiations manage to balance cooperation with competition. In the initial phases of the process, parties compete in an effort to test the strength of the other side and determine their priorities. You should not be surprised to see such competitive communication tactics as threats, manipulation, resistance to persuasion, high opening demands, and attempts to maximize tangible resource gains (Murray, 1986).

Although such tactics indicate strength and take advantage of the anchoring effect of initial offers, they can create a multitude of problems. Over inflated demands unrelated to objective criteria can be difficult to modify without losing face. Overt power tactics such as threats and promises can polarize each side, and extremely competitive orientations can undermine trust and result in severe damage to the relationship.

Collaborative negotiation, in contrast, is concerned with the relationship between the negotiating parties and assumes that both parties can gain something from the negotiation. Murray (1986) identified the presumptions of collaborative negotiation:

- The interdependence of both parties is recognized
- Common interests are valued
- Resource distribution is seen as a joint process
- Mutually agreeable solutions are sought. (pp. 179-186)

The challenge in negotiation lies in the ability to vary your strategies, moving from competition to collaboration. Hocker and Wilmot (1991) identified specific communication strategies that can help you manage the delicate balancing act between competition and collaboration:

1. Join with the other
   - use "we" language
   - seek common interests
   - consult before acting
   - nonverbally move closer
2. Control the process, not the person
   - use setting and timing creatively
   - encourage the other to expound fully
3. Use principles of productive communication
   - be unconditionally constructive
   - refuse to sabotage the process
   - persuade rather than coerce
   - refuse to hate the other
4. Be firm in your goals, flexible in your means
   - be provisional—seek alternative means to goals
   - separate content and relationship issues
   - focus on interests, not positions

5. Assume that there is a solution
- invent options for mutual gain
- tackle issues first where agreement is easy
- take issues one at a time
- refuse to be pessimistic (p. 225)

Successful negotiators, Donohue (1981a) found, used more diversity of arguments, gave more offers, denied more faults more frequently, rejected offers more, and changed the topic more frequently than did unsuccessful negotiators. In other words, successful negotiators used a variety of power resources and argumentation strategies. Unsuccessful negotiations, on the other hand, were characterized by matching attack-defend tactics that led to an impasse. As we have said in previous chapters, flexibility is the hallmark of constructive conflict management.

SUMMARY

To be successful in negotiating, you need to recognize when the necessary conditions are present—avoid negotiating when agreement is not the goal of both sides. Similarly, you should make sure you are negotiating with the people who actually have the authority to make an agreement "stick." Successful negotiations require that both sides have the desire and the capacity to reach an agreement.

Successful negotiators are confident of their abilities, but not overly confident. They recognize the factors that can skew their own decision making, considering how they frame issues and process information. Effective negotiators set clear, moderately difficult goals, but they are flexible about the means for accomplishing them. Finally, successful negotiators use a variety of argumentative strategies and power tactics, avoiding mirroring the responses of the other side. They try more things and vary their approaches.

Win/win negotiations are marked by variety. The disputants manage to balance competition with collaboration, moving through a variety of stages from initiation through problem solving to resolution. Win/win negotiations avoid endless attack-defend cycles while focusing on determining each side's interests and priorities. The disputants agree on objective criteria for measuring solutions. Most clearly, successful negotiations involve a good deal of skill on all sides.

DISCUSSION QUESTIONS

1. When was the last time that you had to negotiate something in your organization? What obstacles did you have to overcome in this negotiation?
2. What is your orientation when you negotiate? Do you approach issues in a negative or positive frame?
3. Do you always plan your negotiation strategy before you actually negotiate?
4. What were your interests in your last negotiation? Did you present them to the other side or did you focus on your positions?
5. List criteria for a negotiation you are about to begin. Are these criteria objective and easily identifiable?
6. Are you a competitive or a cooperative negotiator? What are some advantages/disadvantages of your negotiation style?
7. Can you identify the three stages of most negotiations? What are the characteristics of each stage?
8. What are two basic collaborative negotiation techniques that you can use in your next negotiation?

EXERCISES

What follows is a fairly short simulation that will involve participants in applying the concepts in this chapter. Each bargaining unit should be given 15 minutes to plan their negotiating strategy after receiving a description of the vacation home. The actual negotiations usually require about 20 minutes. Those groups that cannot reach agreement within this time frame have usually fallen into stalemate. Comparing the outcomes leads naturally to a discussion of the different negotiation approaches and their consequences.

Description of Vacation Home

1. 1,200 square feet.
2. 3 bedrooms, 2 bathrooms.
3. Kitchen includes dishwasher, oven, and refrigerator.
4. Fully carpeted.
5. Ocean front property.

6. Near transportation centers.
7. Central air conditioning, electric heat.
8. Access to tennis courts, swimming pool, and clubhouse once completed.
9. Stereo/intercom.

Private Information to the Sellers

You and your partners own a one-of-a-kind vacation home. This home must be sold immediately for legal reasons. During the current recession, one of your partners has lost her job and another has decided on early retirement and wants to invest in a franchise operation. Negotiations with the last possible buyers are about to begin.

If the buyers do not buy your home within *30* minutes, the home will have to be relinquished to the court for $50,000. If deadlock ensues, you will end up with $50,000 to split. This amount barely covers your expenses in purchasing the home (i.e., closing costs, legal fees, payments). Any price over $50,000 is, therefore, to your advantage; the more you get, the more you keep.

Examine the description of the vacation home and make a proposal to the buyers. The buyers have had an opportunity to assess the same data and are waiting to hear your proposal. There are no specific market prices for the home because of its newness, but real estate specialists feel that $160,000 would be the absolute maximum that could be asked. You will have to estimate the home's value as best you can. The buyers know nothing of your constraints except the fact that negotiations must end in 30 minutes.

Discuss this matter with your partners and write down the following information before negotiations begin.

1. Asking price. $_____

2. The highest price you believe you can get; the one that would make you feel that you had achieved an excellent deal. $_____

3. The price below which you will personally consider your investment a failure. $_____

4. Your estimate of the buyers' aspiration level;
   the price above which they will feel a sense
   of personal failure. $_____

5. The lowest price you will take if the pressure
   gets very heavy. $_____

Private Information to the Buyers

You and your partners have $150,000 from the sale of property that must be reinvested immediately in order to avoid capital gains taxes. You no longer have time to shop around. Negotiations with the owners of the vacation home are about to begin.

  If you cannot agree on a price within 30 minutes, the IRS will force you to accept a settlement which will leave you with only $50,000 after penalties and taxes. If you agree to purchase the home, all your tax obligations can be deferred until you sell the home. The less you pay for the home, the more you keep of your investment nest egg. The sellers know nothing of your constraints except for the fact that negotiations must end in 30 minutes.

  It is not possible to determine the market price of the home because it is so new. You will have to estimate its value as best you can. Real estate specialists, however, have told you that houses in the area have sold for as little as $60,000 and as much as $160,000.

  Discuss this matter with your partners and write down the following information before negotiations begin.

1. The lowest price at which you believe the
   home can be purchased; the price at which
   you feel an excellent deal has been made. $_____

2. The price above which you will personally consider your performance a failure. $_____

3. Your estimate of the sellers' aspiration level;
   the price below which the sellers will feel a
   sense of personal failure. $_____

4. The highest price you will pay for the home if
   the pressure gets very heavy. $_____

REFERENCES

Douglas, A. (1962). *Industrial peacemaking II.* New York: Columbia University Press.

Donohue, W.A. (1981a). Analyzing negotiation tactics: Development of a negotiation interaction system. *Human Communication Research, 7,* 273-287.

Donohue, W.A. (1981b). Development of a model of rule use in negotiation interaction. *Communication Monographs, 48,* 106-120.

Fishchoff, F., Slovic, P., & Lichtenstein, S. (1977). Knowing with certainty: The appropriateness of extreme confidence. *Journal of Experimental Psychology: Human Perception and Performance, 3,* 552-564.

Fisher, R., & Ury, W. (1981). *Getting to yes: Negotiating agreement without giving in.* Boston: Houghton Mifflin.

Folger, J.P., Poole, M.S., & Stutman, R.K. (1993). *Working through conflict: Strategies for relationships, groups and organizations* (2nd ed.). New York: HarperCollins.

Hocker, J.L., & Wilmot, W.W. (1991). *Interpersonal conflict* (3rd ed.). Dubuque, IA: Wm. C. Brown.

Holmes, M. E. (1992). Phase structures in negotiation. In L.L. Putnam & M.E. Roloff (Eds.), *Communication and negotiation* (pp. 83-105). Newbury Park, CA: Sage.

Korait, A., Lichtenstein, S., & Fishchoff, B. (1980). Reasons for confidence. *Journal of Experimental Psychology: Human Learning and Memory, 6,* 107-118.

Leeson, S.M., & Johnston, B.M. (1988). *Ending it: Dispute resolution in America.* Cincinnati: Anderson Publishing.

Lewicki, R.J., & Litterer, J.A. (1985). *Negotiation.* Homewood, IL: Irwin.

Liebert, R.M., Smith, W.P., Hill, J.H., & Keiffer, M. (1968). The effects of information and magnitude of initial offer on interpersonal negotiation. *Journal of Experimental Social Psychology, 4,* 431-441.

Mier, R., & Gills, D. (1992). Historic civil rights case offers many lessons in negotiation. *Negotiation Journal, 8,* 339-346.

Murray, J.A. (1986). Understanding competing theories of negotiation. *Negotiation Journal, 2,* 179-186.

Neale, M.A., & Bazerman, M.H. (1985). The effects of framing and negotiator overconfidence on bargainer behavior. *Academy of Management Journal, 28,* 34-49.

Neale, M.A., & Bazerman, M.H. (1991). *Cognition and rationality in negotiation.* New York: The Free Press.Putnam,

Putnam, L.L. (1985). Bargaining as organizational communication. In R.D. McPhee & P.K. Thompkins (Eds.), *Organizational communication: Traditional themes and new directions* (pp. 129-148). Newbury Park, CA: Sage.

Putnam L.L., & Roloff, M.E. (1992). Communication perspective on negotiation. In L.L. Putnam & M.E. Roloff (Eds.), *Communication and negotiation* (pp. 1-17). Newbury Park, CA: Sage.

Roloff, M.E., & Jordan, J. (1989). *Strategic communication within bargaining plans: Forms, antecedents, and effects.* Paper presented to the second biannual Conference of the International Association for Conflict Management, Athens, GA.

Roloff, M.E. & Jordan, J. (1992). Achieving negotiation goals: The "fruits and foibles" of planning ahead. In L.L. Putnam & M.E. Roloff (Eds.), *Communication and negotiation.* (pp. 21-45). Newbury Park, CA: Sage.

Yukl, G.A. (1974). Effects of situational variables and opponent concessions on a bargainer's perceptions, aspirations, and concessions. *Journal of Personality and Social Psychology, 29,* 227-236.

▶6

Using Third Parties to Resolve Conflicts

INTRODUCTION

In this chapter, we continue our discussion of formal methods for managing conflict by explaining third-party interventions. We focus first on mediation, and then describe arbitration and litigation. Only mediation allows you to maintain some control over the final outcome. Arbitration and litigation remove the resolution from your final control, turning decision making over to a third party.

There are times when you need to turn to outsiders to help you deal with conflicts in the workplace. As the following case study indicates, third parties are called into conflict situations when the participants become locked in rigid positions. Third parties are a way of working through this deadlock.

Case Study 6.1: The Disputed New Van

At Agawam Auto Supply, the delivery drivers are excited about the new delivery van that management is going to buy. Each driver feels that he deserves the van. However, with only one new van and two drivers, somebody is going to be disappointed. Bill Freeman has been with Agawam for five years and though he has seniority over the other driver, Steve Turner, his driving record is not as good as Steve's. Bill has had three minor accidents over the last two years, and Agawam has had to pay for increased insurance coverage to keep Bill on the road. However, all the mechanics at the local garages like Bill because he is more knowledgeable than Steve about auto parts, having been a mechanic himself.

When Peter Anderson, the owner of Agawam Auto Supply, calls Bill and Steve into his office to announce who is going to get the new delivery van, Steve Turner announces, "If I don't get the new van, I'm going to quit!" At the same time Bill Freeman says, "I have the better driving record regardless of seniority. I deserve the new van!" Peter is in a bind. He likes both drivers; they are hard workers and know their routes well. However, the fact remains that only one of the drivers is going to get a new delivery van. A friend of Peter's who works at the community mediation center tells him that this dispute is one that could probably be handled through mediation. However, Peter has no idea what mediation is and is a little reluctant to make use of it to resolve this dispute.

Ignorance of mediation is one of the major obstacles to its use in the United States. Nevertheless, mediation is a viable alternative for disputes in the workplace and a process Peter would be wise to consider. In this chapter we discuss using professional mediators. Most managers, however can be trained as mediators and might find the steps outlined here helpful for resolving disputes in their organization. After explaining the steps in the mediation process, we briefly summarize the steps involved in arbitration and litigation.

WHAT IS MEDIATION?

Mediation is the oldest form of dispute resolution in the United States and was introduced to Western culture by the Christian Church, Quakers, and Mennonites. Mediation is the intervention by a neutral third person or persons in a dispute to facilitate the joint decision-making process between disputants who are unable to reach an agreement as a result of differing goals, values, and perceptions (Keltner, 1987). The mediator doesn't make decisions for the disputants; he or she empowers them to reach an agreement that they both deem acceptable, which, in turn, fosters a sense of responsibility for implementing the joint decision. The mediator is not a judge or arbitrator who imposes a settlement after considering all the facts. Mediators are not concerned in determining guilt or innocence, only in helping the disputing parties arrive at a solution where both parties are "winners."

Probably one of the biggest obstacles to mediation is the belief that it, like other forms of dispute resolution, produces a winner and a loser. The legal system in the United States naturally produces adversaries, and people usually expect a winner and a loser in the settlement of a dispute. Getting people to realize that there are two winners in mediation, and if they agree to the process, *they* will determine the outcome, is not an easy task. However, once people agree to mediation, they will reach an agreement 50 to 80% of the time (Clarke, Valente, & Mace, 1993; McKinney, Kimsey, & Fuller, 1992).

What are the Steps in the Mediation Process?

The following steps summarize the four-phase mediation process.

Introducing the process. The first phase of mediation is essentially an orientation phase in which disputants are not only introduced to the mediator(s), but to the process of mediation. After personal introductions, the mediator explains how the mediation process works. Some common ground rules for mediation include the following:

- each side is given equal time to explain its perception of the problem;
- each individual must agree not to interrupt the other disputant;
- name calling or profanity is prohibited;

- all information disclosed will be kept confidential;
- the mediator will not impose a solution;
- the mediator will at times ask for examples or clarification.

It is crucial for each disputant to agree to these ground rules before the mediator moves into the next phase. Without an agreement on these rules, the disputants most likely will not be able to agree on a solution to their dispute.

The most difficult task the mediator faces is convincing the disputants of the power they have to resolve their dispute. The empowering nature of mediation is something some might not feel comfortable with, especially if they are used to having their disputes solved through organizational sanctions. Anger and hostility often characterize disputant's attitudes, and many conflicts have a long and complex history. Disputing parties usually have had a long time to develop inflexible attitudes, emotional postures, and the "I'm right" attitude as in the dispute over the delivery van. Both Bill and Steve feel that there is no question over who should get the new van. Mediators must cut through negative emotions and focus on creating an atmosphere in which each disputant knows that he or she will be treated with dignity and respect (McKinney, Kimsey, & Fuller, 1992). Once it is made clear that they will be empowered to manage their dispute, the disputants are able to move on to the next phase of mediation in which the nature of the conflict is discussed.

Defining the conflict. Each disputant is given the chance to tell their perception of the conflict. The mediator encourages the parties to get all the facts and feelings into the open, and attempts to focus on the underlying causes of the conflict. While one disputant is telling his or her side of the dispute, the other is told to take notes on any issues they would like to contest from the first disputant's side of the conflict. Taking notes helps prevent disputants from interrupting the other party and keeps the disputants focused on the issues at hand.

Frequently the mediator must help the disputants to identify the interests that define their positions (Fisher & Ury, 1981). As we mentioned in chapter 5, getting the disputants to define their perspective of the dispute involves asking the simple question "Why?" In our case study, for example, both Bill and Steve state their positions: "I deserve the new van." However, their interest in the new van stems from its working air conditioning. Whoever gets the new van will no longer have to swelter in traffic.

The van will thus make their jobs a little more comfortable. If people are encouraged to discuss the reasons behind their positions, they often do not appear as irrational as they seem when they present their position in the dispute.

Careful listening is a crucial part of the mediator's role. While listening to each disputant's story, the mediator needs to apply the skills we mentioned in chapter 2. Specifically, the mediator:

- is careful to separate facts from inferences
- paraphrases each disputant's story for accuracy
- gives the other disputants a chance for "rebuttal" after each disputant's story,
- listens for areas of possible agreement between disputants

Mediators must also be able to tell the difference between facts and inferences. The mediator will hear many sides of the dispute, but must keep focused on the factual nature of the dispute, not on the inferences. For example, in the scenario about the new van, it is a fact that only one person can drive the van. It is an inference by the disputants that receiving the new van will demonstrate that they are a more deserving employee. In this instance, a mediator would look for the factual nature of the dispute. Inferences about who "deserved" the new van would be put aside to discuss the real nature of the dispute: the lack of air conditioning in the older van.

Statements of inference include conclusions, opinions, attitudes, and evaluations—statements about the unknown based on the known. Statements of facts are first-hand reports that simply describe and do not evaluate what one sees and hears. Haney (1967) offered suggestions for distinguishing facts from inferences. Statements of fact can only be made after observation, must approach certainty, and can only be made to the extent of the observer's competency and capabilities. Inferences can be made at any time, go beyond observation, and are limited only by one's imagination.

The communication skills we identified in chapter 2 are the tools of a mediator's trade. Besides active listening, restating, clarifying, and summarizing are crucial (McKinney, Kimsey, & Fuller, 1992). Perception checking involves the mediator feeding back the emotions of the message to the speaker, for example, "You seem to be upset that Brian would get the new van. Is this right?" Paraphrasing involves the mediator offering feedback to the speaker regarding content of the disputant's message. In our van example, the mediator might paraphrase by asking, "So, you have not had a new van in three years. Is that correct?" Restatement is used to avoid a problem in communication called *bypassing*, in which the listener assumes that he or she understands the meaning of the speaker's message without checking with the speaker.

Clarifying is a skill in which the mediator asks questions to gain further information about a point. A mediator might ask the disputing drivers for a clarification such as, "When you say that your van is no good, do you refer to the working order of the van or the fact that it lacks air conditioning?" Finally, an effective mediator summarizes each disputant's story to make sure that he or she has fully understood the disputant's view.

Solving the problem. The problem-solving phase begins when the mediator tries to identify the key issues presented, summarizing them and dealing with them one at a time. The summary should detail specific issues as well as points of agreement between the disputants. In the example regarding the new delivery van, we would want to reach an agreement that would ensure that each driver would be working with a van having adequate air conditioning. If the disputants are unwilling to work cooperatively, a reminder of the long-term costs of failing to reach an agreement is sometimes an effective tool in problem solving. A technique used by many mediators is simply to ask each disputant, "How do you think we could settle this dispute?" Sometimes, once a disputant is forced to hear the "other side" of the story during the definition of the conflict, they are more apt to look for cooperative solutions.

Specifically, the mediator should:

- identify key issues defining the conflict
- prioritize issues
- focus on areas for possible agreement
- periodically provide a summary of progress

It is sometimes necessary to meet with each disputant individually and explore ideas privately. This is known as a *caucus*, and is usually used when an impasse is reached.

Disputants will often want to rush toward reaching a solution before they understand the nature of the problem. This is termed *solution centeredness* (Maier & Solem, 1962), and can result in faulty decision making as we mentioned in chapter 3.

The classic example of solution centeredness is presented by Fisher and Ury (1981) regarding an orange desired by two sisters. When the mother learns that each daughter wants an orange, she slices the orange in half and gives a piece to each daughter. One daughter proceeds to take the rind to use for a pie and throws away the rest of the orange; the other sister throws away the rind and eats the orange.

If the mother had focused on the problem of *why* each sister wanted the orange, she could have given each girl what she wanted without wasting any of the orange. By simply awarding one employee the new van without hearing both disputants' reasons for wanting a new van, a similar mistake could be made. Without knowing that Bill's main concern is simply having a van with air conditioning, management might overlook the possibility of giving Steve the new van while installing air conditioning in Bill's older van.

In solving the problem, the mediator guides the disputants in generating as many possible solutions for each of the issues identified, beginning with the easiest issue. If disputants are able to agree on minor issues, they are more apt to agree on much larger issues. Although some early concessions may appear to be insignificant, they can effectively be used to build a climate of agreement. Smith (1982) termed this the *foot-in-the-door phenomenon*, in which disputants comply with a small initial request and work on larger commitments later.

The problem-solving stage ends when all issues—all points in contention in the dispute—have been discussed and an acceptable resolution is achieved. The disputants are then ready to reach the final stage of mediation, where they will put their agreement in writing.

Implementing the agreement. The purpose of the final phase of the mediation process is to bring the mediation session to a close and provide documentation for the agreement. The agreement should specify who agrees to do what, when, and how. The language of the agreement should be as specific as possible so there is little chance for a misunderstanding. The agreement should be signed by both the disputing parties and the mediator(s). For example, an agreement of the new delivery van dispute might look like this:

> The management of Agawam Auto Supply agrees to award the new delivery van to Steven Turner. At the same time Mr. Turner receives the new van, Bill Freeman's van will go into the garage to have air conditioning installed in his van. While Mr. Freeman's van is in the garage, he will be given a rental van to drive that is equipped with air conditioning. Additionally, Steven Turner agrees that since he is receiving the new delivery van, Bill Freeman's delivery route to Springfield (the most distant garage on Agawam's delivery route) will be given to Steven Turner.

In order for any agreement to work, each disputant should understand that the agreement is essentially a contract, and that there might be certain penalties (agreed on in the mediation) levied against any party who violates this contract. Moore (1986) outlined the criteria for the success of a written agreement. They should be (a) cost efficient; (b) simple enough to be easily understood, yet detailed enough to prevent loopholes that cause later procedural disputes; (c) realistic in their demands on or expectations of the parties, and (d) able to withstand public scrutiny.

What Are the Advantages of Mediation?

This four-phase process provides a unique environment for dealing with any psychological resistance inherent in a conflict. Successful conflict management can only take place when the disputing parties are willing to redefine the dispute and engage in constructive dialogue. To empower the disputing parties to address the issues in the dispute with evidence and sound arguments, some kind of intervention to reduce the difference perceptions must first occur.

Initially, the dispute must be reframed from a stance of blaming the other party to one of understanding. The disputants usually see the other as the sole source of their discomfort and anxiety and feel justified in voicing their frustrations with this individual. It is a natural human tendency for people to feel justified in voicing their anger toward those whom they judge to be responsible for their own misery and unhappiness. The first phase of mediation is to build credibility between the disputants and the mediator—the mediator wants the disputants to trust the process of mediation. If the disputants are to be empowered by the process of mediation, they must realize that each side has something to gain in managing their conflict and it can be done without a "winner" and a "loser."

In the stage of defining the problem, the advantage of the disputants' having to listen to the other disputant's view of the conflict, the reframing process begins. Information sharing empowers the disputants to make changes in their evaluations of the other party and issues involved in the dispute. Listening to the other person's perception of the dispute begins an understanding process that can reduce psychological resistance to change. Rather than an individual perspective on the dispute, the disputants now have a joint understanding of the conflict that greatly increases the chances for successfully managing the dispute. In the new delivery van example, the drivers learned the reasons behind each other's position: air conditioning in their delivery vans.

Another scenario involves two employees arguing over who gets the largest office after their office is remodeled. Both of the disputants' stances are "I want that office." Through defining the problem, however, each disputant learns the reasons for the other disputant's stance on the issue. Employee A learns that employee B wants the office because it is near a door, allowing him to slip outside and smoke during a break. Employee B learns that employee A wants the office because she needs the extra space for her recently acquired desktop-publishing system. Although such knowledge does not always lead to a resolution, it gives each disputant a better understanding of the nature of the conflict. The collaborative decision making in mediation yields solutions that are more apt to be implemented by the disputants as opposed to solutions given to them by one person (Maier, 1967).

Despite the obvious benefits of having organizational conflicts mediated, such an approach may not be appropriate for all disputes within organizations. Organizations with strong unions that have relied on arbitration might not be willing to change established dispute resolution methods. Many employers might not be comfortable empowering subordinates to settle their disputes. However, as Stamato (1992) noted, no one process is likely to be appropriate for handling all types of disputes in organizations (i.e., sexual harassment and discrimination), but mediation addresses a variety of needs in the management of organizational conflicts: the need for confidentiality and flexibility, the need for a variety of remedies that reach beyond individual parties, and, most of all, the interest of both parties in avoiding the cost, delay, and exposure associated with litigation.

How can You Implement Mediation in the Workplace?

The process of mediation can easily be implemented in the work-place without excessive cost and training. One of the central beliefs of mediation is that it works best when used to manage disputes with individuals who have an ongoing relationship rather than a one-time encounter. This is what can make media-tion so effective in the workplace. It can help employees who have to continue their interactions on a day-to-day basis. Most com-munity-based mediation centers can provide free training,[1] and employees could receive compensation for attending these train-ing sessions. Several considerations need to be addressed in order for mediation to be effective in organizational settings.

Who Should Be Trained as Mediators?

There are many different mediation models, and most can be learned by anyone with good communication skills in listening, problem solving and decision making (McKinney, Kimsey, & Fuller, 1992). Two aspects crucial to mediation—empowerment and neutrality—indicate which employees should be trained as mediators. Because empowerment is crucial to the success of mediation, employees must not feel that the mediator is one from whom they are used to taking orders. Mediators should be people from different departments *who mediate outside of their normal workplace.* If a disputant agrees to enter into a mediation in the workplace, he or she might not feel empowered when the media-tor is a supervisor. Additionally, if the mediator is someone whom the disputants know well, they might think that neutrality on behalf of the mediator might be impossible. Ideally, the mediator should be from the same organizational level as the disputants to avoid seeing the mediator as an authority figure.

When Should Mediation Take Place?

Another key aspect of mediation—confidentiality—needs to be considered when scheduling mediations in the workplace. If two employees are having problems, it might not be in the best inter-est of the company to schedule mediations during the day. If

---

[1]Most community mediation centers offer a training program lasting 20 hours in which students are trained in all phases of mediation.

employees are noticeably absent from their work stations to take part in mediation, the confidential aspect of mediation may be lost. In most community mediation centers, mediations are done during evening hours. This is probably the best time for a couple of reasons: (a) employees will not miss work, and (b) the scheduling of mediation after normal business hours can help keep the confidentiality of the mediation process.

The biggest obstacle to mediation is convincing the disputants that mediation is a "win/win" process in which they will have the power to decide the outcome. The adversarial process of dispute resolution is so ingrained in American culture that most people feel that only those disputes having a winner and a loser can be settled. Convincing workers that this is not always the case may prove to be the biggest challenge in introducing mediation in the workplace. Clearly, the process of mediation is a successful conflict management tool that should not be overlooked.

WHAT IS ARBITRATION?

The remainder of this chapter focuses on two other forms of third-party interventions—arbitration and litigation. We only provide a brief summary of those formal dispute-resolution techniques that involve individuals *outside* of the organization. Once a dispute goes beyond negotiation or mediation, it is time to submit it to a neutral third party who renders an enforceable decision through either arbitration or litigation.

Unlike mediation, if disputants decide to have a conflict settled by a professional arbitrator, they may lose control of the final decision rendered, but they will still have some say in the way a dispute is settled. Each disputant may set criteria under which the arbitrator must operate, but they are still allowing the arbitrator to make the final decision. In the workplace, arbitration is used most often for contract disputes, and arbitrators are usually selected from a list of arbitrators from the American Arbitration Association—a clearinghouse for arbitrators located in Washington D.C. with regional offices throughout the United States.[2]

---

[2]Further information about arbitration may be obtained from the American Arbitration Association, 140 West 51st Street, New York, NY 10020-1203. Phone: (212) 484-4000, FAX: (212) 765-4874.

Arbitration is "a neutral third-party decision-making intervention that is less legalistic and more informal . . . whereby a neutral third party makes a decision regarding a dispute when the parties to the conflict are unable to resolve the struggle themselves" (Keltner, 1994, p. 151). Most arbitration follows a process in which (a) there is a joint selection and payment of an arbitrator, (b) objective standards on which the decision of the arbitrator is based, and (c) procedural rules to be applied by the arbitrator (Goldberg, Green, & Sander, 1985). The American Arbitration Association requires that arbitrators under their sanctions reach a decision in 30 days or less. The disputants also determine if the decision by the arbitrator is nonbinding or binding. In nonbinding arbitration, a party dissatisfied with the decision of the arbitrator can take the award of arbitration to court. When an arbitrator makes a decision in binding arbitration, the decision is usually final, although federal and state courts have shown increasing willingness to review arbitration awards (Leeson & Johnston, 1988).

What are the Steps in Arbitration?

Like mediation, arbitration follows a series of steps that guides both the disputants and the arbitrators. The first step, *agreement to arbitrate*, has two classifications: The first is called a future-dispute arbitration in a contract whereby the parties agree that any disputes encountered in the future will be settled by arbitration. The second classification in an agreement to arbitrate is the submission of an already existing dispute to arbitration. A sample of an agreement to arbitrate is set forth by the American Arbitration Association:

> We, the undersigned parties, hereby agree to submit to arbitration under the Commercial Arbitration Rules of the American Arbitration Association the following controversy: (cite briefly). We further agree that the above controversy be submitted to (one)(three) arbitrator(s). We further agree that we will faithfully observe this agreement and the rules, and that we will abide by and perform any reward rendered by the arbitrator(s) and that a judgment of the court having jurisdiction may be entered upon the award. (American Arbitration Association, 1991, p. 6)

The second step in arbitration is the *selection of the arbitrator*. The American Arbitration Association maintains a National Panel of Arbitrators consisting of more than 50,000 arbitrators throughout the world. The disputing parties receive a list of arbitrators in their area from the American Arbitration Association. The parties then have 10 days to study the list (biographical information about arbitrators is included), and remove the names of individuals whom they do not want to serve as the arbitrator(s) in the dispute. In the event that the disputing parties cannot agree on the selection of arbitrators, the American Arbitration Association will make an administrative appointment of an arbitrator, but will not chose from those deleted from the list.

Preparation for the hearing, the third step in arbitration, begins when the case administrator contacts all parties to schedule a date for the arbitration hearing that is convenient to all individuals. In preparing for the hearing, the disputants are encouraged to do so carefully because the key determinant in the arbitrator's decision is the facts and exhibits presented. The American Arbitration Association guarantees individuals involved in the dispute the right to counsel or other qualified individuals who can be authorized to represent a disputant.

The final step in arbitration is the *presentation of the case*. Although arbitration shares many characteristics with litigation, it is, among other differences, a much less formal process. First, the arbitrator makes his or her decision based on a quantum of proof; he or she does not have to be convinced beyond a reasonable doubt. Arbitration is private, has no jury, and admits hearsay evidence. The presentation of the case in arbitration follows a set procedure:

1. Each side is allowed to make an opening statement that describes the nature of the controversy and what they are trying to prove. It is customary for the claimant to proceed first followed by the respondent, unless the arbitrator feels it is necessary for the respondent to go first.

2. Each party presents a discussion of the solution desired that should fall within the arbitrator's power and authority to grant.

3. Witnesses are introduced in a systematic order to help clarify the nature of the controversy. The American Arbitration Association prefers the testimony of witnesses to hearsay evidence.

4. Each side presents a closing statement that should be a summary of the case that they have presented and a refutation of points made by the opposition. (American Arbitration Association, 1991, pp. 8-14)

The award presented by the arbitrator is binding and may not be changed by the arbitrator once it is made. Courts will rarely allow cases into litigation that have been arbitrated. However, in some disputes it is necessary to proceed to litigation when mediation and arbitration are not suited to handle the dispute.

WHAT IS LITIGATION?

When all other dispute resolution processes fail, the one remaining choice is litigation. However, disputants lose all control in the final decision and turn it over to the judicial system. Litigation is America's formal dispute-resolution process; it begins with the filing of a lawsuit and terminates with a dismissal of the suit or the enforcement of a judgment entered in the suit. We focus on civil procedures because this is where most disputes in the workplace are litigated.

What are the Steps in the Process

The process itself has five phases: pretrial, trial, post-trial, appeal, and enforcement. The *pretrial phase* of litigation begins with the filing of a lawsuit that focuses on applicable law and narrowing the factual and legal issues that separate the disputing parties. The person filing the dispute is called the *plaintiff*, and the person against whom the suit is filed is the *defendant*. The plaintiff might seek *general damages* to cover items like hospital bills, lost income, or property damage. The plaintiff might also seek *punitive damages*, which are designed "to impose monetary punishment upon persons who act in a reckless manner toward fellow human beings" (Calvi & Coleman, 1989, p. 2).

The defendant is issued a summons in which he or she must answer the charges brought against him or her. The defendant then has the choice to file a *demurrer* to dismiss the complaint, yet is it infrequently granted. If the defendant does not answer the summons, he or she could be issued a default *judgment*, in which the plaintiff is entitled to the damages sought in the dispute.

During *discovery*, each side learns the strengths and weaknesses of the other side's case by using one of three possible scenarios. The more common type of discovery is a *deposition*, in which each witness appears at the office of one of the lawyers to answer questions about the case. The witness is under oath, and a stenographer records everything said. A witness might be questioned in the presence of both lawyers. Sometimes witnesses' depositions are so strong that the case is dropped.

Another form of discovery is called an *interrogatory*. This is a series of written questions directed toward one of the parties, which may be held in contempt of court if it does not answer. The third form of discovery involves the presentation of physical evidence that is in the possession of one of the parties. A judge may issue a *subpoena duces tectum* requiring the person to appear in court and present this evidence (Calvi & Coleman, 1989). Surprisingly, over 90% of all lawsuits filed end in the pretrial phase (Leeson & Johnston, 1988).

The *trial phase* is the one with which most Americans are familiar. Trials follow a set, chronological order. The first step is the selection of the trier of the facts; either a judge or a jury. If a jury is used, the members are selected from a pool of possible jurors called a *venire*. After the jury is selected, they are sworn in and are *impaneled*.

The lawyers provide their opening statements, which may be seen as the "blueprints" of the cases they hope to build. The plaintiff's case is presented first and witnesses are called for *direct examination*. After the plaintiff's lawyer is finished, *cross examination* by the defendant's lawyer begins. The plaintiff's lawyer may question his or her witness again under *redirect* and the defendant's lawyer may *recross-examine* the plaintiff's witness. The plaintiff has the burden of establishing the validity of the complaint.

The defendant's case is presented next followed by rebuttal by both sides. Closing arguments are presented by each lawyer, and the jury (if there is one) is instructed by the judge of the application of the relevant law. The last aspect of the trial phase is deliberation and the verdict by either the judge or jury. If there is a jury, they must come to a consensus of either guilt or innocence.

During the trial, there are one of three burdens of persuasion that the plaintiff must meet depending on the type of case being presented: *preponderance, clear and convincing,* and *beyond a reasonable doubt.* Preponderance is the least difficult burden of persuasion to satisfy. It simply means that the evidence presented is stronger than the evidence presented against it. Preponderance is the burden of persuasion in most civil cases. Clear and convincing means that the evidence presented by the plaintiff is enough when considered with the evidence presented against it, and it is used in cases of civil commitment to a mental hospital or holding a person in contempt of court. In criminal cases, the burden of proof is beyond a reasonable doubt, meaning that the jurors have no doubt about guilt or innocence.

The *post-trial phase* determines if a fair trial was held and post-trial motions generally focus on questions of law. A losing party may move for a new trial if they feel the law was not correctly followed, or if they feel that one of the judge's rulings was incorrect. A decision may be appealed to the next level of court and is usually granted during the *appeal phase*, whereas an appeal to a higher appellate court is usually done at the discretion of the higher court. The losing party usually has 30 days to file for an appeal or he or she will waive the right to appeal.

The *enforcement phase* entails steps that are taken to secure enforcement of the outcome of the suit. Getting to the enforcement phase is a long and costly process and, in most cases, should be the last dispute resolution process employed in the workplace. People go to court, as opposed to some other form of settlement, because:

1. they overestimate their chances of winning;

2. they become emotionally charged and need to retain their moral aggression against the other party;

3. they prefer judicial procedures to negotiation;

4. they wish to demonstrate a firm attitude to the other side;

5. they have interests that transcend the specific case, such as getting a clear-cut decision in a test case that raises the issue of long-term importance;

6. their lawyers have a professional interest in finding out what the law is and an idealistic interest in furthering law and justice;

7. they are fighting over an indivisible interest that affords no compromise solution (zero-sum dispute). (Goldberg, Green, & Sander, 1985, p. 152)

SUMMARY

In this chapter we discussed formal techniques for conflict management that all involve the use of third parties to resolve disputes. Mediation provides the disputants with the most control over the final outcomes. A mediator serves to facilitate the process; the disputants resolve their differences themselves. Maintaining control over the final outcome and involving the disputants in the process are the main advantages of mediation. Although mediation cannot resolve all kinds of disputes, it is appropriate when employees will continue to be interdependent in the future. This formal dispute-resolution technique places equal emphasis on maintaining the relationships as well as resolving the conflict issues.

Arbitration and litigation, on the other hand, move the decision making for dispute resolution to neutral third parties outside of the organization. Arbitrators are most typically chosen by the disputants and make binding decisions about how the conflict will be resolved. Litigation involves a lengthy process involving the judicial system. These formal dispute-resolution techniques focus solely on deciding issues, often to the detriment of the relationships between those involved in the conflict. For this reason, these conflict-resolution techniques are usually a last resort.

DISCUSSION QUESTIONS

1. Can you identify any recent disputes that could best be managed by mediation?
2. Can you identify any disputes in your organization that could not be resolved through mediation?
3. How do you usually respond to a position of another person that is different from your own?
4. How could you approach a fellow employee in order to convince him or her that mediation might be a good way to manage a dispute that they are having with another employee?
5. What are some types of disputes in your organization that would be best served through litigation? Arbitration?
6. Can you think of any advantages that mediation would have over litigation and/or arbitration for managing disputes in your organization?
7. How could you set up a mediation program in your organization?
8. From a management perspective, how could you convince employees to try arbitration before they try litigation?
9. What has been your experience with the legal system? Has it been a positive or a negative experience?
10. Who would be the best people in your organization to teach mediation skills?

REFERENCES

American Arbitration Association. (1991). *A guide to arbitration for business people.* New York: American Arbitration Association.

Calvi, J.V., & Coleman, S. (1989). *American law and legal systems.* Englewood Cliffs, NJ: Prentice-Hall.

Clarke, S.H., Valente, E., & Mace, R.R. (1993). *Mediation of interpersonal disputes: An evaluation of North Carolina's programs.* Chapel Hill, NC: Institute of Government.

Fisher, R, & Ury, W. (1981). *Getting to yes.* Boston: Houghton Mifflin.

Goldberg, S., Green, E., & Sander, F. (1985). *Dispute resolution.* Boston: Little, Brown.

Haney, W.V. (1967). *Communication and organizational behavior.* Homewood, IL: Irwin.

Keltner, J.W. (1987). *Mediation: Toward a civilized system of dispute resolution.* Annandale, VA: Speech Communication Association.

Keltner, J.W. (1994). *The management of struggle: Elements of dispute resolution through negotiation, mediation, and arbitration.* Cresskill, NJ: Hampton Press.

Leeson, S.M., & Johnston, B.M. (1988). *Ending it: Dispute resolution in America.* Cincinnati: Anderson

Maier, R.F. (1967). Assets and liabilities in group problem solving: The need for an integrative function. *Psychological Review, 74,* 239-249.

Maier, R.F., & Solem, A.R. (1962). Improving solutions by turning choice situations into problems. *Personnel Psychology, 15,* 151-157.

McKinney, B.C., Kimsey, W.D., & Fuller, R.M. (1992). *Mediator communication competencies.* Edina, MN: Burgess International.

Moore, C.A. (1986). *The mediation process: Practical strategies for resolving conflict.* San Francisco: Jossey-Bass.

Smith, M.J. (1982). *Persuasion and human action: A review and critique of social influence theories.* Belmont, CA: Wadsworth.

Stamato, L. (1992). Sexual harassment in the workplace: Is mediation an appropriate forum? *Mediation Quarterly, 10*(2), 167-172.

▶7

Managing Cultural Differences

INTRODUCTION

Conflicts become even more complicated and difficult to manage when those involved come from different cultures. Most of us tend to assume that our habitual ways of perceiving and interpreting the world are "natural" and "universal." We don't recognize our assumptions until our perspective is challenged by those who do not share our basic view of the world. What are legitimate conflict issues? How should differences be expressed? What are effective methods for managing conflict? Our answers to these questions are profoundly influenced by our cultural backgrounds. In this chapter, we examine the role that culture plays in conflict interaction.

145

Because the patterns of shared beliefs we describe can apply to an organization or a nation, we have chosen to move from the general to specific. After defining what we mean by culture, we focus on factors that make a difference between people of different national cultures. We then look more specifically at differences that emerge between co-cultures within organizations. Our goal is to help you recognize the implicit assumptions that members of the dominant culture in the United States bring to the conflict process.

WHAT IS CULTURE?

"Culture," Hofstede (1984) asserted, "is the collective programming of the mind which distinguishes the members of one category of people from another" (quoted in Samovar & Porter, 1991, p. 51). The essential function of this collective programming is to allow us to make sense of the world by helping us to structure our behaviors and our interpretations of others. We can think of cultural beliefs and values as the social ties that bind members together by creating a common perspective on reality or a common worldview. Whatever the level of generality, when we examine cultural dynamics we are looking at the patterns of shared meanings about what "ought" to be that develop among group members.

These culturally influenced ideas of what "ought" to be constrain our thought patterns, limit our emotional displays, and shape our behaviors during conflict (Ting-Toomey, 1985). Most problematically, cultural differences cloud our judgments, leading us to inaccurately diagnose the other side's motives and intentions. Most of us tend to use our own frames of reference when we try to understand the actions of others. When we don't recognize how the "other" is looking at a different piece of the whole, it is difficult to find common ground. In such instances, it becomes all too easy to negatively evaluate the other side. We all have a tendency to be ethnocentric, to view our own culture as the best.

Thus, the first step in managing cultural differences is to *cultivate an attitude of openness*, accepting that other ways of viewing the world are different rather than wrong. In order to do this, you must first be aware of North American cultural assumptions about what it means to be an effective manager and a competent communicator. After discussing differences that emerge across national boundaries, we focus more specifically on differences that emerge within organizations between the members of the dominant culture and those in the minority. Our goal, once again, is to help you become more aware of your own cultural assumptions.

WHAT DIFFERENCES MAKE A DIFFERENCE?

We cannot discuss all of the cultures in the world in a single chapter, nor provide an exhaustive critique of North American culture. We focus only on those assumptions that are most basic and most likely to prompt misunderstandings when North American businesspeople interact with their counterparts from other countries. We must also add the proviso that any generalizations about cultures as a whole are likely to be inaccurate in dealing with individuals. People respond in unique ways, even those who belong to the same culture. As we have mentioned throughout this book, flexibility is key. With these limitations in mind, we will talk about different superior/subordinate role expectations, definitions of competent communication, preferences for methods for conflict resolution, and modes of reasoning. We conclude this section with suggestions for managing cross-cultural negotiations.

Role Expectations

What behaviors make a manager effective? North Americans would probably describe an effective boss as one who asks for input from subordinates, who is technically competent, and who delegates authority. A Mexican might answer the question quite differently. An effective manager dictates to subordinates, is politically well-connected, and protects his or her privileges and turf (Condon, 1985). National cultures shape our expectations about the roles we should play in our professional lives.

  In the following case study, notice how different expectations about the appropriate role of a manager and a subordinate exaggerated the tensions between John Miller and his subordinate, Costa Mitsotakis. Each individual interpreted the other's actions in terms of his own cultural assumptions. The result was a destructive conflict.

Case Study 7.1: The International Project Team

John Miller is a North American manager leading a international project team for a multinational corporation. Costa Mitsotakis, a Greek, is one member of the project team whose specialty is statistical analysis. The following dialogue took place between the Mr. Miller and his subordinate, Mr. Mitsotakis.

CM: *(Knocking on Miller's door) Did you want to talk to me, Mr. Miller?*

JM: *Ah, Costa, yes . . .*
    (Mitsotakis shuts the door and draws the only available chair sitting in front of Miller's desk to within four inches of Miller's knees. Miller, swiveling in his chair, backs up an equivalent distance.)

JM: *It's about the report required by the Ministry of International Trade. How long will it take you to finish it?*

CM: *(Surprised at being asked a question when he had expected to receive instructions from his boss.) I don't know, Mr. Miller. . . . Umm. . . . Do you think?*

JM: *(Interrupting) No, Costa, no! . . . You are in the best position to analyze time requirements. (Feeling the pressure of time deadlines himself, Miller glances at the spreadsheet waiting on his computer, frustrated that he has to do everything because his subordinates refuse to take responsibility). How long do you think it will take you?*

CM: *(Shifting positions in the chair and looking flustered. Mitsotakis thinks: Why does he expect me to guess what's expected? I better tell him something that sounds good.) Well, let's say 10 days.*

JM: *Let's say 15 . . . alright? (Miller looks for signs of agreement, but Mitsotakis avoids direct eye contact and seems expressionless.) Then we have an agreement. You will do it in 15 days.*

CM: *Yes, Mr. Miller*
    (The report in fact needed 30 days of regular work. Thus, Mr. Mitsotakis worked day and night, but at the end of 15 days, he still needed one more day's work.)

JM: *(On his way to another meeting down the hall, Miller stopped in Mitsotakis' office.) Well, Costa, where is the report?*

CM: It will be ready tomorrow. (Mitsotakis turned back to
        the piles of papers scattered on his desk, exasperated.
        Not only had Miller given the wrong orders, but he did
        not appreciate that the job was done in 16 days rather
        than 30).

JM: (Shaking his head as he walked out the door). You
        agreed it would be ready today! I have to get to a meet-
        ing now, but we really have to talk about your inability
        to plan and meet deadlines.

From that day on, the relationship between Costa Mitsotakis and
John Miller became more and more difficult. Three months later,
Costa asked for a transfer to another project (adapted from
Triandis, 1972)

Stewart and Bennett (1991) asserted that North
Americans "often interpret cultural factors as characteristics of
individual personality," ignoring the importance of the social conditioning producing behavior (p. x). In this case, each person
interpreted a cultural difference as an individual failing. Although
the American saw his subordinate as irresponsible, the Greek
saw his boss as lacking in sensitivity. Each operated from different assumptions about how you should deal with those in
authority.

"Authority conception," Borisoff and Victor (1989) wrote,
"may be defined as the degree to which individuals believe those
higher up in the authority chain have the power to influence or
command behavior" (p. 143). Mr. Mitsotakis expected his boss to
exert his power by telling his subordinate what to do. Asking the
subordinate to decide was a sign of the boss's lack of competence. When an authority figure put Costa on the spot, however,
he was compelled to respond with something that sounded good.
In cultures that maintain a relatively high distance between the
powerful and the less powerful, an employee cannot indicate that
what a superior has proposed is impossible. Instead, the employee will attempt the impossible and fail rather than point out the
shortcomings of the one in authority.

Americans, in contrast, expect subordinates to raise concerns and question authority, providing input into the decision-
making process; employees, and not their bosses, are thus held
accountable for outcomes. Rather than focus on the power differences between bosses and their subordinates, Americans tend to
view each other as colleagues and equals. Mr. Miller was disappointed when his subordinates did not "take initiative." He

assumed his subordinates were avoiding responsibility when they were actually acting in accordance with their culture's definition of appropriate subordinate roles.

North Americans tend to minimize the importance of age, seniority, and family or social status as power sources, while these factors are of primary importance in other cultures. "For Americans," Fisher (1980) explained, "technical competence is basic. It is the *position* that supplies the authority for incumbents whose background is an egalitarian society" (p. 21). This orientation reflects a primary American value of individualism. In the United States, you are evaluated in terms of your individual achievements—you are what you do.

In contrast to the United States, which is individualistic, many other cultures are collectivist. Here, your individual identity is the product of your position in a web of social relationships—family, community, and institutional affiliations. You are evaluated in terms of who you are, not what you do. For this reason, in many parts of the world, the "best" person to hire is likely to be a family member. Nepotism is viewed as an effective mechanism for fulfilling personal obligations and for ensuring the trust and accountability of workers. Family ties can be more important than contractual relationships or technical competence (Borisoff & Victor, 1989).

Because individuals in collectivist cultures are defined primarily by their roles within social groups, power comes from the connections you establish with those in positions of authority. In Mexican organizations, for example, what Americans might consider to be personality factors count to a much greater degree. "Mexicans talk of an individual's prospects in terms of his 'ubicacion'—where he is 'plugged in' in the system," Fisher (1980) asserted (p. 23). To delegate is to dilute the power of your connections. Thus, an individual who delegates authority is likely to be viewed as on his way out rather than on his way up.

Similarly, American management practices that reward individual efforts can create problems in other cultures. In a collectivist culture such as that of the Japanese, singling out an individual for praise can be as embarrassing as criticizing them personally. To separate one from the group can result in a loss of face. Promoting a single individual instead of rewarding the group as whole will not encourage others to work harder—it can have the opposite effect.

The role of a group leader can also be very different in other cultures. Americans try to discover *who* makes decisions, according to Fisher (1980), viewing leaders as facilitators who ensure that individuals can voice their opinions freely. The Japanese are confused by this American focus on individual decision makers because Japanese organizations rely on a system of consensus building in which ideas are frequently initiated from the bottom, or at most, the middle level. Fisher (1980) suggested that "direction taking," rather than "decision making" (p. 31), is a clearer way of describing how Japanese organizations function.

Here, the role of a group leader is largely symbolic—to present a united front to the outside. Rather than view decisions as finite activities that individual managers implement, the Japanese perceive an ongoing process of adjusting and modifying according to changing conditions and needs of the parties involved (Fisher, 1980). While Americans are likely to view the consensus decision-making process as slow, implementation after a decision has been made is more rapid (Stewart & Bennett, 1991, p. 64).

Clearly, basic accepted practices of American management such as delegating authority, hiring based on technical competence, and rewarding individual efforts have no equivalents in other cultures of the world. Ironically, the very attributes that make a manager successful in the United States might cause failure in an overseas posting. There are, however, a few simple adaptations that you can make to improve your chances of effectiveness.

A U.S. boss operating in a culture with high respect for power differentials should expect more requests for approval than might be typical in a U.S. organization. Following the proper chain of command is more important in cultures that carefully distinguish between the powerful and less powerful. In addition, you can adapt some American habits such as the use of first names. To individuals from collectivist cultures, the American tendency to use first names and omit formal titles is disorienting because it eradicates the status markers that members of that culture have learned to use in relating to others.

When it comes to more fundamental differences about hiring and decision making, it can be difficult to avoid negative judgements about practices that are so radically different from what you have been trained to do. You can, however, recognize the legitimacy of alternative value systems, without necessarily accepting them. By being aware of the different role expectations, you can make conscious choices about the adaptations you choose to make and avoid the unrecognized problems that plagued Mr. Miller and Mr. Mitsotakis.

Definitions of Effective Communication

In dealing with those from other cultures, we are aware that our languages are different, requiring translation. What we don't recognize as easily are the ways in which language structures perception, guiding us to view the world from a particular perspective. Our language system creates a framework for our perceptions, leading us to pay attention to some stimuli and ignore others.

For example, the common subject/verb structure of the English language imposes a framework for viewing the world in terms of linear causality. The structure of our language emphasizing actor/action/result conditions us to assume that human activity requires human agents. Events don't happen naturally; they require a cause or a human agent that can be held responsible. In the conflict process, this characteristic of our language system encourages our evaluative tendencies, leading us to search for someone to blame.

Americans aim toward the future, and their language allows them to stress planning and project the future in making decisions (Stewart & Bennett, 1991). The future tense in English is more fully developed and frequently employed than in other languages. The Turks, for example, have no future tense, while the Sioux have no words for late or waiting. Zen Buddhists view time as an infinite pool with no past, present, or future. Many cultures have much less faith in an individual's ability to plan and mold the future. For the Spanish, the future is uncertain; thus, while an American might discuss their future plans in terms of "I will," the Spanish rely on the more tentative construction "I may." The Arabic language adopts a similarly tentative attitude toward the future, assuming the future is unknowable because it is in Allah's hands.

In addition, the English language abounds with digital opposites (is/is not; black/white; love/hate). To define a concept in English, users are forced by the nature of the symbol system to chose one of the extreme ends of the continuum. The Chinese language includes a similar subject/verb/object structure, but avoids sharp contrasts by expressing emotions through "complimentary pairs of moderate emotions such as deference and politeness." (Stewart & Bennett, 1991, p. 51). In this sense, Chinese is analogic, fixing a user's attention on the quality of the continuum rather than on polar opposites. Although English is weak in representing gradations of emotions, moods, and relationships, it is precise in representing mechanical and technical processes.

The digital nature of the English language also leads a user to imply opinions when selecting the subject of a question. "How good is the food here?" is a different question from "How bad is the food here?" (Stewart & Bennett, 1991 p. 54). An American is forced to implicitly appraise the food in the question compared to a Portuguese speaker, who would ask, "What is the quality of the food here?" English speakers convey an implicit message in selecting one extreme of the continuum.

Broader cultural differences emerge in how individuals attribute meaning to interaction. Is the meaning of a message contained primarily in the explicit communication (low-context) or is it implicit in the context (high-context) surrounding the verbal language? The distinction can be thought of as the difference between figure and background. What is most important in one culture (the figure) is simply the background in another culture.

In a low-context culture (LCC) such as the United States, individuals rely primarily on the verbal content of a message, placing less emphasis on the meanings contained in the context. North Americans, valuing explicit communication, place great emphasis on learning how to say exactly what you mean. Americans get to the point quickly, avoid long greetings and farewells, and are generally impatient with extended digressions or vivid details illustrating a point. Stewart and Bennett (1991) describe the American direct style as "linear, in which speakers are expected to come to the point by moving in a straight line of logical thought through the subject to a stated conclusion" (p. 157). Other low-context cultures include Germany, Scandinavia, Switzerland, and Canada (Adler, 1992).

High-context cultures (HCC), such as Asian, African, and Native American cultures, on the other hand, interpret messages in terms of the broader context of shared social and cultural assumptions. High-context cultures rely on inferred meaning rather than the literal meanings. A speaker need not present ideas in a linear order as long as a general context is provided. The meaning of a message comes primarily from the implicit understand of the social context and relationships surrounding the parties involved. For members of high-context cultures, what is not said is often as important as what is said.

Obviously, low-context and high-context cultures provide very different definitions of credibility. In low-context cultures, the primary function of verbal messages is to express ideas as clearly and logically as possible. Messages are identified with individual speakers who may be recognized for their ability to influence others. If a message is misunderstood, the fault lies with the sender who failed to use clear language.

In high-context cultures, the primary function of verbal messages is to "enhance social relationships and to downplay the importance of individual speakers" (Samovar & Porter, 1991, p. 3). Responsibility for understanding a message resides more with the receiver, who must interpret the nonverbal and relational cues surrounding an often ambiguous message. In high-context cultures, "an eloquent speaker may be judged as patronizing—acting as if the listeners are incapable of fulfilling their responsibility" (Stewart & Bennett, 1991, p. 158).

Because speaking two languages in the United States is a marker of low status (Stewart & Bennett, 1991), many Americans tend to ignore the subtle role of language in shaping interaction and thinking. Although we translate the words, we are more reluctant to adapt our style of communication. "Americans who believe that 'deep down' everyone appreciates honest directness," Stewart and Bennett (1991) wrote, "will continue to exact a heavy toll of tolerance from their more indirect foreign associates" (p.157). When communicating across cultures, you should be ready to suspend your preference for directness and consider the context and relationships.

There are also a number of factors you should keep in mind when deciding on a translator. Compatibility is the most important characteristic of an interpreter (Samovar & Porter, 1991). You have to feel comfortable with your translator, selecting someone who is not too domineering or too timid. However, this individual must also be acceptable to the people you want to communicate with in terms of family background, religious beliefs, and ethnic identity. Ideally, the translator should be fluent in both the necessary dialect and the specialized language in your field of expertise.

For meetings, you can help your interpreter by briefing him or her on the history of the relationships as well as on the substantive issues at hand. Specifically review the technical terms you intend to use. Ask the interpreter to inform you of cultural differences in eye contact or other nonverbal behaviors that might be important. Be sure to ask about unwritten rules of conversation. For example, to inquire about the wife of a Muslim is impolite, whereas neglecting to ask about a person's family in Mexico would be cold and aloof. Speak slowly enough for the translator to understand, using short sentences. Pause often and look at the audience while you speak, not at the interpreter. Finally, you should prepare greetings and farewells in the foreign language and ask your translator to coach you on correct pronunciation.

Cultural differences also emerge in the nonverbal codes we use—our body language. Americans are moderately expressive in their body language. We are not vivid compared to Mediterranean or Arab cultures, but we are more nonverbally expressive than Asians (Stewart & Bennett, 1991). The Japanese desire to avoid offending the other party leads them to provide few nonverbal clues regarding their responses to spoken messages. Americans, left without feedback about how their messages are being interpreted, have a difficult time knowing when the answer is "no."

In general, however, North Americans view nonverbal codes as being secondary to verbal codes. This means that Americans are not prepared to deal with those from cultures in which the nonverbal code is of primary importance in interpreting messages. Emphatic expression is expected in Arab cultures. As Almaney and Alwan (1982) explained: "If an Arab says exactly what he means without the expected assertion, other Arabs may still think he means the opposite" (p. 84). Emotional displays indicate sincerity and a true concern for the discussion.

These differences in nonverbal codes can function as noise in the communication process, creating subtle tensions. Fisher (1980) delineated some of the nonverbal behaviors that people from other cultures find most distracting in Americans:

> slouching, chewing gum, using a first name too soon, displaying the soles of one's shoes in a respondent's face, forgetting titles, starting speeches with jokes, inappropriate clothing, overly friendly approaches to the opposite sex, speaking too loudly, being too egalitarian with the wrong people, working with one's hands and carrying bundles, and tipping too much. (p. 54)

Although these behaviors are frequently not mentioned, they can create an underlying level of stress that exaggerates conflict interaction. Effective cross-cultural interaction requires that you be a careful observer of behavior, doing what you see others around you doing, and questioning your own assumptions about "acceptable" behavior.

Preferences for Managing Conflict

With their emphasis on social relationships, high-context cultures rely more on conflict resolution methods such as consensus, accommodation, and avoiding. Vagueness and strategic ambiguity will be employed during times of tension, allowing individuals to withdraw from positions that might cause them to lose face. An Asian speaker may abruptly change the subject without an obvious reason if he or she feels the listener does not agree with the ideas, or if his or her feelings are hurt. Often, concealment is necessary to maintain the complex webs of relationships in the social context.

North Americans, in contrast, rely more on confrontation, a method that might be considered shameful in Japanese society because it ignores the social context. Low-context cultures focus on revealing the areas of disagreement rather than concealing them to allow unanimity. As Ting-Toomey (1985) explained:

> LCC individuals can fight and scream at one another over a task-oriented point and yet be able to remain friends afterwards; whereas, in the HCC system the instrumental issue is closely tied with the person that originated the issue. (p. 77)

American preferences for direct and explicit statements of the areas of disagreement can violate strongly held social norms in other cultures that do not differentiate between conflict issues and conflict parties.

Different cultural definitions of credibility lead to different criteria for selecting negotiators. American negotiators are usually selected because of their technical competence in the subject of the negotiation or in the process of negotiation. Other cultures use criteria such as power, authority, gender, and status. In Mexico and many countries in the Middle East, negotiators are selected because of their rhetorical skills and are nearly always men. A Chinese negotiator serves as a go-between, having little authority to deviate from initial positions except through additional conferences, which Americans view as a waste of time.

Americans are also unique in their concern with the methods and procedures used to manage conflict. Focusing on explicit communication, they place great faith in written contracts. Collectivist cultures do not make a similar separation between substantive issues and procedures for organizing problem solving. Agendas and other formal procedures serve ritualistic functions rather than being vital to the process. The Japanese, for example, are skeptical of written contracts, viewing them as a sign of a lack of trust in the relationships. Americans can thus be accused of evasiveness when they insist on resolving procedural matters before turning to substantive issues. In fact, some argue that the whole notion of specifically scheduled negotiating session is purely Western (Fisher, 1980).

Definitions of a "fair" deal are culturally based as well. North Americans commonly operationalize fairness through a 50-50 split. The Mexicans view compromise in more negative terms—integrity and dignity are matters of personal honor that should not be compromised. Similarly, in the Persian language, the word for compromise means "surrendering one's principles" (Samovar & Porter, 1991, p. 240). "To the French," Fisher (1980) explained, "a well-reasoned position does not call for compromise unless the reasoning is faulty" (p. 48). The Chinese, on the other hand, "stress mutual interests and believe that the advantaged party (i.e., the Americans) should gain less without protest" (Nadler, Nadler, & Broome, 1985, p. 97). The Chinese definition of fairness revolves around issues of responsibilities rather than compromise procedures. Germans and Eastern European cultures leave little room for compromise. Scandinavians tend to make offers or bids that reflect what they believe to be a fair price—they expect the other party to recognize and accept its fairness. Arabs, on the other hand, tend to inflate initial prices, hoping to haggle before settling on an acceptable price (Samovar & Porter, 1991, p. 241). Clearly, terms like "fair" are determined by cultural values.

Reasoning Patterns

Americans show a marked preference for factual/analytic reasoning rather than intuitive/synthetic modes. "Analysis," Stewart and Bennett wrote, "dissects events and concepts into the pieces which can be linked in causal chains and categorized into universal criteria" (p. 41). Analytic thinking presupposes an objective reality that can be accurately known and verified by systematic observation of the "facts." Facts are assumed to be objective, divorced from the observer, and, therefore, reliable because they are not grounded in an individual perspective or a particular context.

Procedural knowledge is important because it is through the procedures used to measure facts that reality becomes apparent. Reliance on linear progression of premises and practical justifications, and a focus on expert opinion and hard facts, spring from an assumption of an objective reality understood through analysis. A factual/analytic thinker assumes that the facts speak for themselves and that logic leads to the right conclusion.

Factual/analytic thinkers rely on such words as: explain, clarify, define, meaning, because, then, consequently, therefore, and in order to. A factual/analytic mode of thinking is particularly effective when considering questions such as, "What is it?" and "How do we get there?" (Casse & Deol, 1985).

Intuitive/synthetic thinking is more dominant in Asian cultures and a number of subcultures within the United States. This mode of reasoning presents a clear contrast to the factual/analytic mode. Intuitive/synthetic thinking relies on analogies, metaphors, and similes. A synthetic reasoning pattern does not separate reality from the perceiver, assuming that reality cannot be divorced from the prism of language and experience through which it is apprehended and mediated (Anderson, 1989). Relying on general principles, contemplation, and intuition, intuitive/synthetic thinking lacks "the power of precise analysis and abstract classification, but it excels in identification by evoking concreteness, emotion and commitment to action" (Stewart & Bennett 1991, p. 44).

In such a perspective, knowledge cannot be divorced from the social processes used to generate knowledge. Such thinking, Stewart and Bennett asserted, "involves a high degree of sensitivity to context, relationships, and status" (p. 42). Interpretive perspectives take precedence over "objective" facts. An intuitive/synthetic thinker assumes that facts are the product of interpretation rather than objective reality. The key words that indicate such a mode include: principles, ideas, essential, wrong, right, good, and bad. This mode of thinking is effective when confronted with questions such as, "What could it be?" and "How important is it?" (Casse & Deol, 1985). When it comes to conflict, Ting-Toomey (1985) clarified the contrast between these different reasoning modes by explaining that analytic thinkers tend "to engage conflicts from the mind," whereas intuitive thinkers "tend to approach conflicts from the heart" (p. 81).

Each mode of reasoning has its advantages. The key is to recognize that we don't all think alike. Your mode of reasoning might be diametrically opposed to that of the other side. We suggest that you understand different thinking modes, learn to identify the mode of reasoning on the other side, and adapt your tactics accordingly. We have included, in the appendix to this chapter, a survey that can help you identify your preferred modes of reasoning.

Casse and Deol (1985) offered the following advice for dealing with those employing a factual/analytic reasoning pattern:

- Be precise in presenting your facts.
- Refer to the past (what has already been tried out, what has worked, etc.).
- Go from the facts to the principles.
- Document what you say.
- Use logic when arguing.
- Look for causes and effects.
- Analyze the relationships between the various elements of the situation or problem.
- Be patient.
- Analyze various options with their respective pros and cons. (p. 67)

When dealing with individuals employing an intuitive/synthetic reasoning process, on the other hand, you should be prepared to adapt your style in the following ways:

- Focus on the situation as a whole.
- Project yourself in the future (look for opportunities).
- Tap the imagination and creativity of your partner.
- Be quick in reacting (jump from one idea to another).
- Build upon the reactions of the other person.
- Establish a sound relationship right at the outset.
- Show your interest in what the other person is saying.
- Identify his or her values and adjust to them accordingly.
- Appeal to your partner's feelings. (p. 67)

HOW CAN YOU MANAGE CROSS-CULTURAL DIFFERENCES

Given all these differences, how can we successfully manage conflict across national boundaries? While there are no magic solutions, we have adapted a number of Casse and Deol's (1985) suggestions to provide a list of things you can do to improve your chances of effectiveness:

1. Planning is critical. You should learn about the culture you will be dealing with and adapt your tactics to avoid minor irritants such as the use of first names.
2. Recognize that cultural stereotypes are misleading. While you should plan, you also need to be flexible, because what you expect is not likely to happen.

3. Check for understanding from time to time, keep your pace slow and make liberal use of questions. Language is both an important link across cultures as well as a barrier. You should recognize the limitations of your language system and provide opportunities to get feedback on how you are being perceived.

4. Recognize the importance of nonverbal communication in intercultural communication. Be careful about the meanings you convey, consciously or unconsciously.

5. Accept the "other" as different, not wrong. Feelings of contempt, mistrust and suspicion hinder the communication process. Suspend your judgements. (p. 133)

HOW CAN YOU MANAGE DIFFERENCES BETWEEN CO-CULTURES?

Although cultural differences are most apparent when comparing national cultures, different beliefs about what "ought" to be develop among subcultures within organizations. A white, male head of the accounting department is likely to view the effectiveness of an advertisement quite differently than an African American, female advertising account executive. As we mentioned in earlier chapters, an individual's specialized function can lead them to develop habitual ways of perceiving and responding to the world. Similarly, a person's gender or ethnic heritage can shape perceptions of the world.

Most typically, an organization's dominant culture promotes a "managerial perspective" in which individual differences tend to get washed out. (Putnam & Mumby, 1993). What remain after this socialization process are the values most compatible with those of dominant culture. In the corporate world, analysis is privileged over synthesis, and facts are preferred to feelings. All too often, intuitive/synthetic modes of reasoning are relegated to the realm of the "weak," the "illogical," and "the disruptive" (Putnam & Mumby, 1993, p. 36). In these preferences, corporate organizations reflect broader cultural norms.

Because it takes more effort to challenge emotional norms than it does to fake an acceptable display, most individuals feign emotions that they might not feel in order to conform to organizational norms. The contrast between feigned and felt emotions creates stress that can emerge as horseplay or childish behavior. In some cases, emotional stress leads to sabotage. Waldron and

Krone (1991) found that emotional control within organizations reduced upward communication, made employees fearful of protesting perceived unjust actions, and sometimes resulted in inadequate justifications for company actions.

Devaluing the role of emotions, particularly during times of conflict, negates the individual and ignores the positive role of emotions in creating a sense of connection and group cohesion. By privileging factual/analytic thinking over intuitive/synthetic thinking, most corporate executives implicitly overlook questions such as, "What could it be?" and "How important is it?" However, these questions are a necessary element in change efforts.

The dominant value structure in many corporate organizations can be particularly problematic for women and people of color, whose life experiences may be more at odds with the officially prescribed "managerial perspective." African Americans, for example, are likely to employ different definitions of "reasonable" argumentation than members of the dominant culture. Rather than ignore alternative modes of reasoning, it pays to understand them.

Allowing greater freedom for assertion and self-expression, African American cultural norms encourage individuals to approach argumentation as advocates, testing perspectives through challenging each other's ideas. For blacks from the inner cities, the views expressed about specific issues cannot be separated from the core values that a person holds. To claim that you do not have an individual point of view is insincere. Thus, African Americans will probe to discover "where a person is coming from" in an effort to understand the perspective determining the specific view (Kochman, 1981).

Members of the dominant culture, on the other hand, approach argumentation as spokespeople, not advocates, assuming that the truth exists in objective reality distinct from the individual perceiving that truth. The dominant culture encourages an impersonal mode of expression lacking in displays of emotion. To those accustomed to different reasoning patterns, the dispassionate, analytic reasoning patterns of the dominant culture can appear cold and impersonal at best, and deliberately deceptive at worst.

Although whites are likely to assume that heated arguments indicate a closed mind, blacks view animated argumentation as a sign of commitment to the process. "Blacks," Kochman (1981) explained, "believe that personal differences can only be worked out by engaging in struggle, even if the arguments resulting from such an engagement become heated and abusive" (p.

58). The absence of affective displays among African Americans indicates that the gap between disputants is widening rather than being resolved.

Neutrality is viewed with skepticism by African Americans, who use such low key modes only when they feel threatened and forced to suppress what they really feel because they are in the minority. Dispassionate argument in situations without risk is viewed as cheating because:

> It withholds from the group an attitude that might cause the prevailing view to be modified, and is thus considered subversive of a process in which ideas are validated to the extent that the best thoughts of everyone have been entered and tested against each other. (Kochman, 1981, p. 23)

In many ways, African American cultural expectations about persuasion reflect intuitive/synthetic reasoning modes more than factual/analytic modes.

Some researchers have argued that different reasoning patterns also explain gender differences. Empirical research on the different conflict-resolution styles of males and females is quite contradictory. Some studies find significant differences between males and females, while an equal number find no difference in individual behavior (Borisoff & Victor, 1989). We can conclude, however, that although women have learned a managerial perspective, they have also paid a price in terms of emotional dissonance.

What, then, can you do to manage the differences between co-cultures? Whether you are a member of the majority or the minority, you can try to avoid the assumptions and behaviors that block authentic communication. Adler (1992) identified a number of common mistakes that organizational members make in perceiving the "other" side.

If you are a member of the majority culture, you can promote authentic relations by recognizing that differences do make a difference. Members of the dominant culture assume all too often that differences should not affect performance. However, different ways of viewing the world will lead to different methods for acting. As we asserted in the beginning of this chapter, accepting that different is not necessarily inferior is the first step.

Second, don't assume that all members of a co-culture will always welcome being included in the majority culture. Telling a woman that her work is "as good as any man's" might not be perceived as a compliment. Some members of co-cultures would prefer to have their differences appreciated rather than overlooked. You should not assume that the open recognition of differences may embarrass minority members. They need only look around the room to know they are different. It can frequently take more energy to deny differences than it does to acknowledge them.

In acknowledging differences, however, you should take care to avoid the stereotypic complaints minority members hear all the time. Don't assume that minorities are using their situation to take advantage of the majority, or that they are "overly sensitive." Recognize that even "liberal" members of the majority are not necessarily free of biased attitudes, particularly when it comes to implicit assumptions about preferred modes of reasoning.

In terms of your specific behaviors, you should avoid interruptions, condescending behavior and too-easy expressions of friendship. Many members of minority co-cultures cringe when they hear the phrase, "Some of my best friends are . . ." This phrase frequently serves as the preamble to a stereotypic label. Finally, avoid talking about, rather than to, the minority members who are present.

If you are a member of a minority co-culture in your organization, you should also try to avoid making assumptions that block authentic relationships. Not all members of the majority have the same attitudes about minority members. There are some majority members who are really trying to understand those with a different cultural perspective—not all majority members will let you down in a crunch.

In terms of specific behaviors, minority members sometimes err by confronting even minor incidents of discrimination too early and harshly. Confrontation is not the only way to change a situation. Rejecting all offers of assistance can be as destructive as simply giving answers that the majority members want to hear. Finally, by isolating themselves, some minority members make it difficult for majority members to learn about different cultures.

Adler (1992) offered suggestions that minority and majority members can use to promote authentic relations:

- Treat people as individuals as well as members of a culture.
- Demonstrate an interest in learning about other cultures.
- Listen without interrupting.
- Take risks (for example, being first to confront differences).

- Express concerns directly and constructively.
- Stay with and work through difficult confrontations.
- Acknowledge sincere attempts (even clumsy ones) to understand and support members of other cultures.
- Deal with others where they are, instead of expecting them to be perfect.
- Recognize that interdependence is needed between members of majority and minority cultures. (p. 51)

Because gender and cultural differences can be threatening, many people try to pretend that the differences don't exist. We suggest that in American organizations it is usually better to talk about differences rather than ignore them. Pretending that we are all alike depersonalizes all of us. We suggest that you review the suggestions in chapter 2 on how to clarify your own feelings and respond productively to other peoples' emotional displays.

SUMMARY

When you look at the subtlety and variety of cultural differences, you can marvel that conflict is not more prevalent that it is. Different role expectations, assumptions about competent communication, appropriate methods of conflict resolution, and modes of reasoning all contribute to the complex mix of cross-cultural interaction. Hopefully, you can see why it pays to never assume anything during conflict interaction. The other party might have a radically different orientation toward the world than you do. You thus need to probe to discover their perspective and listen carefully to what is and is not said. Ask questions, label your views as tentative rather than absolute, and recognize that your own implicit assumptions are not universal.

DISCUSSION QUESTIONS

1.   What is the expected role of the manager in your organization? How is this expectation related to the cultural makeup of your organization?
2.   Does your organization value and reward individualism? What specific practices encourage or discourage individualism? Is this an effective way for your organization's goals to be achieved?

3. Do you always consider the context and relationship of any message that you send to your employees? Have there been any conflicts in your company because of a failure to consider these two parts of a message?

4. Describe a nonverbal behavior by a fellow worker that you find disconcerting. Is there a cultural basis for this behavior?

5. Are there more intuitive or more analytical thinkers where you work?

6. What steps do you take to learn about the different cultures in which you do business?

7. Are emotions devalued in your organization? How do you deal with "emotional" employees?

EXERCISES

Reasoning Styles: A Self-Assessment Exercise. From Pierre Casse and Surinder Deol. *Managing Negotiations: Guidelines for Trainers and Negotiators.* Washington, DC: SIETAR International, 1985, pp. 54-58. Reprinted with permission of SIETAR International & Intercultural Press (out of print).

Please respond to this list of statements in terms of what you believe you do when interacting with others. Base your answers on your typical day-to-day activities. Be as frank as you can.

For each statement, please enter on the score sheet that follows the number corresponding to your choice of five possible responses given below:

1. If you have NEVER (or very rarely) observed yourself doing what is described in the statement.

2. If you have observed yourself doing what is described in the statement OCCASIONALLY, BUT INFRE-QUENTLY; that is, less often than most other people who are involved in similar situations.

3. If you have observed yourself doing what is described in the statement about AN AVERAGE AMOUNT; that is, about as often as most other people who are involved in similar situations.

4. If you have observed yourself doing what is described in the statement FAIRLY FREQUENTLY; that is, somewhat more often than most other people who are involved in similar situations.

5.   If you have observed yourself doing what is described
      in the statement VERY FREQUENTLY: that is, consid-
      erably more than most other people who are involved
      in similar situations.

Please respond to each statement using number 1-5 (see
above). Use score sheet.

1.   I focus on the entire situation or problem.
2.   I evaluate the facts according to a set of personal values.
3.   I am relatively unemotional.
4.   I think that the facts speak for themselves in most sit-
      uations.
5.   I enjoy working on new problems.
6.   I focus on what is going on between people when
      interacting.
7.   I tend to analyze things very carefully.
8.   I am neutral when arguing.
9.   I work in bursts of energy with slack periods in
      between.
10.   I am sensitive to other people's needs and feelings.
11.   I hurt people's feelings without knowing it.
12.   I am good at keeping track of what has been said in a
      discussion.
13.   I put two and two together quickly.
14.   I look for common ground and compromise.
15.   I use logic to solve problems.
16.   I know most of the details when discussing an issue.
17.   I follow my inspiration of the moment.
18.   I take strong stands on matters of principle.
19.   I am good at using a step-by-step approach.
20.   I clarify information for others.
21.   I get my facts a bit wrong.
22.   I try to please people.
23.   I am very systematic when making a point.
24.   I relate the facts to experience.
25.   I am good at pinpointing essentials.
26.   I enjoy harmony.
27.   I weigh the pros and cons.
28.   I am patient.
29.   I project myself into the future.
30.   I let my decisions be influenced by my personal likes
      and dislikes.
31.   I look for cause and effect.

32. I focus on what needs attention now.
33. When others become uncertain or discouraged, my enthusiasm carries them along.
34. I am sensitive to praise.
35. I make logical statements.
36. I rely on well-tested ways to solve problems.
37. I keep switching from one idea to another.
38. I offer bargains.
39. I have my ideas very well thought out.
40. I am precise in my arguments.
41. I bring others to see the exciting possibilities in a situation.
42. I appeal to emotions and feelings to reach a "fair" deal.
43. I present well-articulated arguments for the proposals I favor.
44. I do not trust inspiration.
45. I speak in a way that conveys a sense of excitement to others.
46. I communicate what I am willing to give in return for what I get.
47. I put forward proposals or suggestions which make sense even if they are unpopular.
48. I am pragmatic.
49. I am imaginative and creative in analyzing a situation.
50. I put together very well-reasoned arguments.
51. I actively solicit others' opinions and suggestions.
52. I document my statements.
53. My enthusiasm is contagious.
54. I build on others' ideas.
55. My proposals command the attention of others.
56. I like to use the inductive method (from facts to theories).
57. I can be emotional at times.
58. I use veiled or open threats to get others to comply.
59. When I disagree with someone, I skillfully point out the flaws in the other's argument.
60. I am low-key in my reactions.
61. In trying to persuade others, I appeal to their need for sensations and novelty.
62. I make other people feel that they have something of value to contribute.
63. I put forth ideas that are incisive.
64. I face difficulties with realism.

65.   I point out the positive potential in discouraging or difficult situations.
66.   I show tolerance and understanding of others' feelings.
67.   I use arguments relevant to the problem at hand.
68.   I am perceived as a down-to-earth person.
69.   I go beyond the facts.
70.   I give people credit for their ideas and contributions.
71.   I like to organize and plan.
72.   I am skillful at bringing up pertinent facts.
73.   I have a charismatic tone.
74.   When disputes arise I search for the areas of agreement.
75.   I am consistent in my reactions.
76.   I quickly notice what needs attention.
77.   I withdraw when the excitement is over.
78.   I appeal for harmony and cooperation.
79.   I am cool when negotiating.
80.   I work all the way through to reach a conclusion.

Reasoning Styles Score Sheet

Enter the score you assign each question (1,2,3,4, or 5) in the space provided. Please note: The item numbers progress across the page from left to right. When you have all your scores, add them up vertically to attain four totals. Insert a "3" in any space left blank.

1. _____	2. _____	3. _____	4. _____
5. _____	6. _____	7. _____	8. _____
9. _____	10. _____	11. _____	12. _____
13. _____	14. _____	15. _____	16. _____
17. _____	18. _____	19. _____	20. _____
21. _____	22. _____	23. _____	24. _____
25. _____	26. _____	27. _____	28. _____
29. _____	30. _____	31. _____	32. _____
33. _____	34. _____	35. _____	36. _____

37. _____ 38. _____ 39. _____ 40. _____

41. _____ 42. _____ 43. _____ 44. _____

45 _____ 46. _____ 47 _____ 48. _____

49. _____ 50. _____ 51 _____ 52. _____

53. _____ 54. _____ 55. _____ 56. _____

57. _____ 58. _____ 59. _____ 60. _____

61. _____ 62. _____ 63. _____ 64. _____

65. _____ 66. _____ 67. _____ 68. _____

69. _____ 70. _____ 71. _____ 72. _____

73. _____ 74. _____ 75. _____ 76. _____

77. _____ 78. _____ 79. _____ 80. _____

IN: _____ SYN: _____ AN: _____ FA: _____

REFERENCES

Adler, R.B. (1992). *Communicating at work: Principles and practices for business and the professions.* New York: McGraw-Hill, Inc.

Almaney, A.J., & Alwan, A.J. (1982). *Communicating with the Arabs: A handbook for the business executive.* Prospect Heights, IL: Waveland Press.

Anderson, J.W. (1989). A comparison of Arab and American conceptions of "effective" persuasion. *The Howard Journal of Communication, 2*(1), 81-114.

Borisoff, D., & Victor, D.A. (1989). *Conflict management: A communication skills approach.* Englewood Cliffs, NJ: Prentice-Hall.

Casse, P., & Deol, S. (1985). *Managing intercultural negotiations: Guidelines for trainers and negotiators.* Washington, DC: Sietar International.

Condon, J.C. (1985). *Good neighbors: Communicating with the Mexicans*. Yarmouth, ME: Intercultural Press.

Fisher, G. (1980). *International negotiation: A cross-cultural perspective*. Yarmouth, ME: Intercultural Press.

Hofstede, G. (1984). *Culture's consequences: International differences in work-related values*. Newbury Park, CA: Sage.

Kochman, T. (1981). *Black and white styles in conflict*. Chicago: The University of Chicago Press.

Nadler, L.B., Nadler, M.K., & Broome, B.J. (1985). Culture and the management of conflict situations. In W.B. Gudykunst, L.P. Stewart, & S. Ting-Toomey (Eds), *Communication, culture, and organizational processes* (pp. 87-113). Newbury Park, CA: Sage.

Putnam, L.L., & Mumby, D.K. (1993). Organizations, emotion, and the myth of rationality. In S. Fineman (Ed.), *Emotion in organizations* (pp. 36-57). Newbury Park, CA: Sage.

Samovar, L.A., & Porter, R.E. (1991). *Communication between cultures*. Belmont, CA: Wadsworth.

Stewart, E.C., & Bennett, M.J. (1991). *American cultural patterns: A cross-cultural perspective*. Yarmouth, ME: Intercultural Press.

Ting-Toomey, S. (1985). Toward a theory of conflict and culture. In W. Gudykunst, L.P. Stewart, & S. Ting-Toomey (Eds.), *Communication, culture, and organizational processes* (pp. 71-87). Newbury Park, CA: Sage.

Triandis, H.C. (Ed.), (1972). *The analysis of subjective culture*. New York: Wiley.

Waldron, V.R., & Krone, K.J. (1991). The experience and expression of emotion in the workplace: A study of a corrections organization. *Management Communication Quarterly, 4*, 287-309.

▶8

Finetuning Your Conflict-Management Strategies

The superior man sets his person at rest before he moves; he composes his mind before he speaks; he makes his relations firm before he asks for something. By attending to these three matters, the superior man gains complete security.
—Confucius.

INTRODUCTION

Our basic premise throughout this book has been that conflict is an inevitable and natural part of any workplace. Differences will emerge between people who have to work together on a day-to-

171

day basis. These differences can spark creative thinking and stimulate change or consume time and energy, reducing productivity and lowering morale. What makes the difference in creating positive outcomes is how people manage their interactions.

Surviving conflict at work involves accepting that "IT" is going to occur, and when it does, you have entered the organizational equivalent of the Twilight Zone. No one person is in control of the course of events. We cannot predict the consequences of our actions with any precision, nor can we easily discern the motives of the others involved. The unexpected is quite likely to happen because conflict episodes are complicated and often ambiguous. We find ourselves asking, "What's going on here?" Our normal categories for dealing with the world don't seem to fit any more and we have to discover new ways of interacting.

Our goal in this book has been to help you make more informed choices about what *is* under your control—your own responses to conflict. Those who have less trouble dealing with conflict have learned to focus their energies, making astute judgments about when the pain of conflict is worth the effort and potential costs. We hope we have given you a clearer understanding of how to create "wiggle" room, discovering what is possible and productive for you in different contexts.

To conclude this book, we summarize the five principles that have organized our discussion of details:

1. Understand the Nature of the Beast
2. Know Yourself
3. Consider the Context
4. Create Options for Acting
5. Understand the "Other" as Different, not Deficient.

Understand the Nature of the Beast

In chapter 1, we focused on sharpening your analytical abilities, describing the subtle and complex dynamics often involved in conflict interactions. We defined what conflict is and identified some of the myths that surround conflict interaction. We highlighted the individual roots of conflict in our need to manage our images and our tendency to mirror behaviors, while describing how organizational constraints such as specialized roles, ambiguous lines of authority, and scarce resources contributed to the mix.

Although conflict is usually stressful, it can be constructive if it prompts a reexamination of current practices and focuses attention on systemic problems inhibiting performance and generates news ideas without permanently destroying ongoing relationships. Conflict interaction involves everyone in a delicate balancing act of competing with each other while still needing to coordinate activities. We can't easily walk away from many disputes at work, and thus have to learn to cope.

We suggested that you look at actual interaction patterns to determine when the pain is worth the effort. Constructive conflict interaction is marked by flexibility; people's behaviors and the issues change. Destructive conflict, on the other hand, involves continuing cycles of attack, defend, and regroup to fight another day. Adversaries remain the same even when the issues change, and outside parties are drawn into the dispute.

When you find yourself locked in destructive conflict cycles, we suggested that you change your patterns of interaction. Throughout this book, we have emphasized that conflict and change are inextricably linked. Turning conflict into constructive movement toward change has a lot to do with avoiding the trap of habitual, gut-level responses to others. You have to develop the ability to create options in the midst of limitations.

Know Yourself

It's one thing to recognize what causes conflict and distinguish between constructive and destructive outcomes. You must then address how productive or effective your behaviors are. Chapter 2 focused on how you can manage your immediate responses to conflict.

Although you cannot control the outcomes during conflict episodes, you can exercise your right to make ethical choices that are consistent with your personal values and career goals. To clarify your professional and personal goals, we suggested that you ask yourself the following questions:

- What's most important to me in the long term?
- What am I willing to "put on the line?"
- What actions will allow me to sleep at night?
- What actions will allow me to be effective in my job?

Knowing your priorities helps you avoid petty squabbles and save your energies for fundamental issues.

Besides making intelligent choices about when to take a stand, you can also control your responses to the inevitable. You can manage your own talk in ways that increase your chances of creating a productive outcome, maintaining your relationships with your coworkers, and preserving your sanity. The specific skills involve careful listening, maintaining a sharp focus on specific behaviors, and clarifying meanings as you go along. Avoiding "defensive" messages is important as well. These communication skills can help you raise delicate issues and provide constructive feedback to others during conflict episodes.

Finally, monitoring your personal stress levels can help you identify your own "hot spots." Stress reduction and successful conflict management often go hand in hand. By developing personalized coping strategies, you arm yourself to deal more productively with one-to-one conflict interactions.

Consider the Context

Many disputes in the workplace move beyond one-to-one interactions to involve multiple players with a variety of interests. In such conflicts, your responses will be influenced as much by the "personality" of your work unit or organization as by individual personalities. People who work together on a regular basis develop shared, albeit frequently unspoken, understandings about "appropriate" behaviors. Understanding how this group context, or climate, can influence conflict episodes is a necessary survival skill.

In chapter 3, we suggested that you assess the climate in your work unit or team by analyzing the nature of the power relationships, the type of interdependence, the level of commitment, and the degree of supportiveness among team members. Developing a climate that fosters productive responses to conflict can be achieved if you monitor your actions as well as the unspoken assumptions that guide group behavior. We identified group behaviors that can help you determine when a group is avoiding, escalating, or working productively on balancing individual agendas with group goals.

Besides influencing the climate in your work unit by clarifying group goals and hidden agendas, you can take specific steps to help a group accomplish its task as well maintain a sense of group identify. All too often, conflicts in work teams develop because everyone focuses only on information giving and opinion giving, and no one coordinates ideas by clarifying, elaborating, and testing for consensus. It's easy to follow along with what others are saying or make quick jokes to release tension; it's more difficult to equalize participation by gate keeping, standard setting, and talking about feelings. Even if you are not the designated leader of a project team or the manager of a work unit, you can develop communication skills that will help your work teams make effective decisions and develop a climate in which conflict is more likely to result in productive change rather than in stagnation and gridlock.

Create Options for Acting

Responding effectively to conflict, rather than simply reacting to it, involves recognizing that you *do* have choices. If you understand a broad repertoire of both formal and informal conflict-management techniques, you can make better choices among alternatives. You are more likely to survive conflicts at work if you adapt your influence attempts according to the issues, individuals, and situational constraints you face. Chapters 4, 5, and 6 concentrated on different informal and formal conflict-management strategies.

In chapter 4, we discussed informal strategies for managing conflict when you are "in charge," illustrating how power dynamics create undercurrents that shape our behaviors in disputes. Power isn't automatically conferred along with job titles, and it's a mistake to assume that power is a possession some people have and others don't. It's more accurate to view power as a kind of force or energy that springs from the relationships among people, the product of subtle and often unspoken agreements about who gets to do what to whom in what situations.

Although job positions usually imply control over certain resources, actual power is conferred by interaction. Without your conscious or unconscious endorsement, no power move will be effective. A necessary first step in dealing with power dynamics is recognizing your own role in the renewal of power.

You should also attempt to develop a variety of power sources and vary your conflict-management strategies depending on your own strengths and weaknesses and your assessment of the resources of the other side. You can try to control what the issues are, try to control key resources, or appeal to common values. Obvious power moves such as rewards and punishments are easier to challenge than hidden power moves that influence the kinds of problems that emerge needing solutions. Avoiding, accommodating, controlling, compromising, and collaborating can all be effective in different situations.

When influencing others, you also need a good sense of what the "other" values. He or she might not value the same things that you do. In addition, you need to be sensitive to the group climate in your influence attempts. Don't become so focused on an individual that you neglect the impact your actions will have on the overall climate within a work unit. Finally, accept the responsibilities that come with power, balancing your influence attempts with judgement and maturity.

In chapters 5 and 6, we considered more formal techniques for conflict management—negotiation, mediation, arbitration, and litigation. What makes these conflict-management strategies different from others is the fact that communication is more consciously controlled. The exchange of proposals and counterproposals involved in each of these procedures defines differences more clearly than other methods of conflict management in which differences can remain diffused or suppressed. Formal conflict-management techniques make conflict tangible and explicit.

Negotiation, unlike mediation, arbitration, and litigation, does not necessarily involve third parties, and, consequently, is one of the most common techniques for creating agreements across organizational boundaries. To be a successful negotiator, you need to make sure you are dealing with actual decision makers who are interested in coming to an agreement through the process. Negotiations can only produce agreements when both sides have the desire and the capacity to reach an agreement.

Effective negotiators set clear, moderately difficult goals that frame negotiating issues in positive rather than negative terms. They use a variety of argumentative strategies, try more things, and vary their approaches to the issues. They are committed to their goals but flexible about the means for achieving them, probing for the interests behind the stated positions of the other side. Effective negotiators manage to balance competition with collaboration, trying out different behaviors at different stages in the negotiation process. In sum, effective negotiators employ the communication skills we have discussed throughout this book.

However, no matter how skilled you might be in communicating there are times when you must use third parties to resolve a dispute. In chapter 6, we summarized the steps in mediation, arbitration, and litigation. Of the three third-party intervention techniques, mediation allows the disputants the most control for resolving their differences among themselves. A mediator is simply a process facilitator; he or she helps control the communication process so disputants can work through their differences. A mediator sets ground rules and serves as a referee during the process, but they do not make final decisions as an arbitrator does. For this reason, mediation is effective when disputants will have to continue to be dependent on each other.

In some instances, however, arbitration and/or litigation may be the only way to resolve a serious dispute. Some contracts specify formal arbitration in lieu of litigation. An arbitrator is selected by the disputants, hears proposals from each side, and makes final decisions that are usually binding for both parties. The arbitration process is designed to be faster and less expensive than litigation.

When other dispute-resolution techniques fail, the one remaining choice is litigation. When disputants turn to the judicial system, they lose all control over the shape of the final decision. Although litigation might be the only means to resolve differences over core values, it is a costly and a lengthy process. For these reasons, it is a form of third-party intervention that should not be undertaken lightly.

Understand the "Other"

When people become tense during conflict interaction, they tend to perceive the other side in terms of their own fears. Distorted perceptions can become reality, even through these "pictures in our minds" might be based on our fears rather than on the other party's actions. Managing conflict effectively involves uncovering the real needs and interests of "the other." We have suggested throughout this book that you probe, question, listen, and dig beneath the surface of unreasonable actions to truly understand the "other" on their own terms. It's important to cultivate an attitude of openness, viewing the other side as different, not wrong. Constructive conflict is motivated by a concern for the "other" as well as a concern for "self."

Cultural differences make understanding the "other" more difficult, as we explained in chapter 7. Different role expectations, assumptions about competent communication, appropriate methods of conflict resolution, and modes of reasoning all complicate cross-cultural interactions. It is wise to never assume anything about the other side's intentions and motivations—the other party might have a radically different orientation toward the world than you do. You need to listen carefully to what is and is not said. Ask questions, label your views as tentative rather than absolute, and recognize that your own implicit assumptions are not universal.

After reading this book, we hope you can see that conflict is not just a temporary aberration in an otherwise harmonious organizational world. Given the stresses of the modern workplace, it is a marvel that conflict is not more prevalent than it is. Although you alone cannot control outcomes, you can understand the nature of the beast and take steps to increase your chances for survival. Know yourself, consider the context surrounding your actions, develop a range of options for acting, and try to understand the "other" as being different, rather than deficient.

Author Index

Subject Index

.